TOUCH OF
LIGHT

TOUCH OF

LIGHT

The Story of Louis Braille

ANNE E. NEIMARK

ILLUSTRATED BY
Robert Parker

HARCOURT, BRACE & WORLD, INC.
NEW YORK

To Paul . . .

whose own light never wavers

CONTENTS

TOUCH OF
LIGHT

❧ 1 ❧

"WHY IS IT SO DARK?"

The gray stone houses on Touarte Street seemed to sag under the weight of heavy shutters and low, moss-covered roofs. At the foot of the steep cobble-stoned street was Simon René Braille's harness shop. Inside, three-year-old Louis Braille sat on the stone floor, his lap filled with scraps of leather. It was the spring of 1812, in a French village called Coupvray.

Louis looked up at the glossy brown harness on his father's workbench. Then his blue eyes stared longingly at the forbidden rack of tools. "I make a harness, too," he whispered. "Like Papa."

Simon René was winding leather thongs on a wide spool. He must have heard his son's eager words, for he turned sharply and shook his head. "*Non, non,* Louis! You may help with many things, but you must not touch the tools. Remember how sharp they are? I gave you the bits of leather to play with."

Louis picked up a handful of the tiny, irregular pieces. Most of the time, they were his favorite toys. He liked to pretend that they were children walking to Monsieur Becheret's schoolhouse or oxcarts rumbling toward the village square on market day.

Lately he'd been imagining them into French soldiers from Emperor Napoleon's army. But today they just seemed like brown leftover scraps of leather.

"Someday I will be big enough to make a harness, won't I, Papa?" he asked. Again, his eyes rose to the rack of tools.

Simon René smiled and patted the tangled blond curls on his son's head. "Someday you will be a full-grown man, Louis. But perhaps you will not want to make a harness then. That mind of yours is quick enough for learning anything!"

The door of the shop suddenly swung open, and a tall man in city clothes stepped inside. "Monsieur Braille?"

"*Oui,*" Simon René answered. "Can I help you?"

"Indeed you can," the man said. "I was nearly twenty miles out of Paris when the girth strap broke on my horse. I came the few extra miles here, to Coupvray, as I've often heard that there was a master harness maker in town. I wonder if you could put on another strap for me?"

Before his father could do more than nod, Louis had scrambled to his feet and dashed to the wall. Standing on tiptoe, he stretched a hand toward the straps that hung from an iron hook. "Let me get one, Papa! I can do it!"

Simon René brushed off his bulky leather apron. "I'm afraid I must help the gentleman, Louis. You will have to grow a foot higher before you can reach my straps!"

"I wish I could grow right now," Louis said.

The new customer laughed and looked around the neat, stone-walled room. Dark slabs of leather were pulled taut across the ceiling beams, and massive rawhides hung from hooks on one wall. It seemed that every inch of the shop was filled with the warm, pungent odor of curing leather.

"You have a fine place here," the man said. "Perhaps the boy will become as famous a harness maker as his father."

"The little one has brains for more than harnesses," Simon René said proudly. "My older son, Simon, will carry on the trade and tend the farm—as I did after my own father. Louis came along much later than my other three children. Why, when I registered his birth with the deputy mayor—January 4, it was, 1809—I said even then that Louis would be the professor of the family, a man of books!"

The two men left the shop, the fresh girth strap slung over Simon René's shoulder. Louis trailed behind and leaned on the wooden railing outside. He looked down at the horse and wagon on the cobblestones below.

"So how goes the war?" Louis heard his father saying.

"Ah—the rumors are flying," the customer answered. "It's said that our armies are exhausted, that Russia will be too big for them—but, still, Napoleon is driving on."

"We are all very tired of the fighting," Simon René said.

The man nodded. "Over 300,000 of our men in battle. Who knows how many thousands will die?"

Louis frowned. So often lately, he had heard the word *war*—but he didn't understand what it meant. He had asked to look at war, but his brother Simon said that there was no war yet in Coupvray. Then why did everyone talk about it, he wondered.

Jumping away from the railing, he ran back inside to the warm safety of the harness shop. . . .

The leather scraps were once again spread out over the workshop floor. Stooping down, Louis began to arrange them into a pattern, imagining them into reins, a breast collar, and two blinders. He would make a harness of his own, he'd decided—a harness that would be strong enough to hold an ox, that would shine like the tufts of corn silk out in the fields.

But how could he make such a wonderful harness without a knife or an awl? "If I punch a hole the way Papa does," he told himself, "then I can put a real buckle on it!"

Slowly, he stood up. His father's oiled and polished tools seemed to wink at him from the rack: razor-sharp knives, pointed awls, and squat, brown-handled mallets. Couldn't he use one for just a minute—only a minute—and then put it *right back* where it belonged?

His heart was pounding as he pulled the shiny awl from its rack. All of his father's warnings rushed in at him, like a swift wind down the stone chimney of their house. *"Don't touch! Don't touch!"* roared the warnings in his ears. But Louis didn't stop.

With the awl clenched in his fist, he bent over the piece of leather. Punching down as hard as he could, he tried to make the hole that he wanted. But when he lifted up the awl, there was only a tiny dent on the surface of the leather.

He leaned closer. Then he lay on his stomach and peered at the sharp and gleaming end of the tool. His cheeks felt as if they were hot with sun, and there was a strange kind of fluttering in his stomach. If he hurried, he could make the hole before his father noticed that anything was missing. Once more, he lifted the awl—and, once more, he thrust it down with all his might.

It slipped. Suddenly, the point was darting toward

him like an arrow to its mark. Before he could move or even blink, there was a quick and terrible pain in his left eye.

The awl clattered to the stone floor. Louis covered his eyes with his hands and felt the wet, spurting blood. Looking down, he dimly saw the red stains that were oozing out over his clothes. "Papa! Papa!" he screamed. "Mama! Papa!"

Louis's mother had been attending to her chores in the gray stone cottage that was attached to the harness shop. The wooden eating table and benches were scrubbed; the dishes sat snugly in their cupboard; the cabbage soup was beginning to bubble in its iron pot on the chimney hook, thick with chunks of mutton, onions, and beets. The downstairs room was whitewashed and tidy, and the straw sleeping pallets up in the children's garret had been turned over and aired.

But when the sounds of Louis's screams filled the small cottage, Monique Braille's face went suddenly pale, and she gathered up her skirts. Quickly, with nineteen-year-old Catherine and fourteen-year-old Marie following behind, she ran toward the door that opened into the harness shop.

"What is it, Mama?" asked Catherine. "What's happened?"

Monique found that she could hardly push the

words from her tightened throat. "It's Louis," she
gasped.

Out in his father's vineyards where he was culti-
vating the grapes, Louis's brother, seventeen-year-
old Simon, heard the anguished cries like the faraway bleating of a wounded lamb. He, too, left his
work and dashed toward the house.

But it was Simon René who first reached his
young, injured son. Sweeping the boy up into his
arms, with the cries of "I'm sorry, Papa, I'm sorry!"
muffled against his chest, he ran with Louis into the
house. The family gathered around in shock and
terror, for both father and child were stained with
the still flowing blood.

"It's his eye," Simon René told them hoarsely. "We
must find someone to help."

But the doctors from Coupvray and neighboring
towns had all gone off to war, and so the Brailles
called in an old herb woman. Monique stayed in the
garret where Louis lay and wiped her own eyes with
the edge of her apron as Simon René and the woman
climbed the stone stairway.

"Please," Monique asked, "do you think you can
heal him?"

The old woman bent over the straw pallet and
clucked her tongue. "Poor little one," she said.

The afflicted eye was bathed with lily water, and
the bleeding finally seemed to stop. "I'll never do it

again," Louis kept sobbing. "It hurts too much. I'll always mind Papa."

"Hush, now," the old woman scolded. "You must try not to cry. I'm putting on the bandages, and you'll get them too wet." Then she turned to the parents. "Change the covering often," she explained. "And make sure that your son stays here in the darkness until he's better."

"Oh, we will be very careful," Monique said.

But in spite of the family's loving care, Louis's eye did not heal well. A week passed, and deep within the cut the bleeding continued and infection set in. Lily water was not the answer to such an eye injury, but in Coupvray in 1812, there were no other answers.

Several weeks after the accident, the bandages were removed. Louis's eye was raw and swollen and streaked with purple. He rubbed his other eye in order to see better, but the infection was spread by his fingers, and soon his good eye was burning, too. Day after day, as he lay in the garret or sat by the hearth downstairs, he tried to rub away the dark coating that was painted over everything he saw. Why were colors so gray, he wondered, and faces so flat and plain?

One sunny morning as his mother woke him for breakfast, Louis asked, "Why is it so dark, Mama? Is there a storm coming?"

"But it's a beautiful day," Monique said. "Can't you see the sun, Louis? Why, it's as yellow as the checks on my apron!"

Louis shook his head. "Where?" he said. "Where is the sun, Mama? How can it shine when I don't see it?"

By nightfall, Monique and Simon René knew that there was never to be another shiny sun in the sky for little Louis.

He would ever after live in the darkness—a darkness more black than the blackest night—for their beloved child was blind.

2

"TELL ME ABOUT

THE GRASS"

Louis held tightly to Catherine's hand as she guided him along the cobblestoned street. He had begged to go for a walk with his sister, but now he was not so sure that he liked the walking after all. Before the darkness had come, Catherine would take him with her to the washhouse near the brook, and he'd carry a bundle of clothes without dropping even *one* piece, and she'd tell him stories about giants and big ships and some of the things she'd read about in books.

Now, the outside of his house seemed almost like the inside—all dark and kind of scary, and not a bit like it used to be.

He remembered running in the grass by the brook before the darkness had come, when he could just

throw off his shoes and the grass under his toes
would tickle, when he could run ahead of Catherine,
and just run and run and run.

He wrinkled his forehead and tried to remember
the color of grass. But what did green *look like?* He
could almost remember. Then, just when he seemed
to have the idea of green, he could only think and
think of black.

"Catherine," he said suddenly. "Tell me about the
grass."

His sister looked down at the small, serious face
by her side. "Well," she said, in as gay a voice as she
could muster, "the best thing about grass is the soft
cushion it makes for all the feet in the world. Big
feet and little feet. People feet and animal feet. Even
bug feet, too! And the second best thing about grass
is the way it smells after a rainfall. Why, I'll make
you a promise, Louis. The next afternoon that it
rains, you and I will go outside and smell the grass.
You'll see—I mean, you'll find out—just how nice it
smells."

They walked on, the sister guiding her brother's
awkward steps—one arm around his waist, the other
holding his hand. But as they neared the bottom of
Touarte Street, a noisy group of children blocked
their way.

Catherine paused and tightened her grip on
Louis's waist. Then she watched as a square cloth

bag was tossed back and forth between the excited boys and girls.

Louis heard the thud of the bag, followed by a rush of tiny clicking sounds. "What's that, Catherine? What are they doing?"

"They're playing catch with a beanbag. Mama made one for you once, remember?"

"*Oui!*" Louis said. Suddenly, he pulled away from his sister and stumbled forward. "Throw it to *me!*" he cried. "Throw it to *me!*"

There was an abrupt halt to the shouting and laughter. A strained silence fell over the breathless children, and only a large spotted dog continued to bark and pant at the heels of the black-haired boy who now held the bag.

The boy, whose name was André, seemed confused. Looking from Louis to Catherine, he dug his fingers into the beanbag and waited uneasily on the edge of the street.

Quickly, Catherine came to the rescue. Bending down behind Louis and stretching her arms out alongside his, she called, "Throw it, André! We can catch it!"

Cautiously, André tossed the bag in Louis's direction. Catherine grabbed her brother's wrists, and as the bag swung toward them, she pushed his hands inward until they clamped around the small, lumpy square of cloth.

"There!" Catherine said. "We did it!"

Louis's face was flushed. "Can I play with them now?" he asked.

Catherine looked up at the children and understood the meaning of the many pairs of eyes that wouldn't look back. "Not this afternoon," she said. "Mama and Papa will be worried about us."

Louis didn't answer. He let his sister guide him the rest of the way home, but as they entered the cottage, he said, "I know they don't want to play with me. They can still see things, can't they, Catherine?"

His sister unbuttoned his sweater and helped him take it off. "You'll be like the bean seeds that grow, Louis. They can't see things under the ground, where it's dark, but nature helps them to grow very strong and tall. Then, one day, they've made a path right out of the darkness. You will be helped to find a path, too, someday."

Louis stood solemnly by the doorway. "I don't want to be like the beans," he said.

Sometimes it was young Simon who tried to make the smiles come back to his little brother's face. When there were too many frustrating moments— when Louis grew impatient at needing to be led about the cottage, at not being able to see the new tassels that his father wove for the harnesses, at hearing the shouts of neighborhood children who played games that he could not join—Simon would play a game of his own with Louis.

Hoisting the boy up onto his shoulders, Simon would strut through the house, letting Louis touch the tops of doors, the high stones on the fireplace, the thick slabs of leather that were strung from ceiling beam to ceiling beam inside the harness shop.

And before long, Louis's laughter would bubble up again. Simon would stop by the staircase to the garret and say, "Tell me what you can feel up there, sailor! Your ship almost reaches to the sky!" And Louis would fling out his hands with delight, rubbing his fingers over the heavy railing.

At supper, the family sat on stools and benches around the table. And while Louis painstakingly learned to feed himself, there was always someone near to wipe up a spilled glass of milk or a few slices of carrots that tumbled down onto the floor.

He was carefully included in the evening conversation. In the midst of talk about the farm or a wedding that was to take place in town, one of the Brailles would be sure to say, "And what about you, Louis? I bet you learned something special today, didn't you?"

The talk would stop while Louis thought back over his morning and afternoon. He might be able to tell how he'd played with the leather shapes that his father had given him and how he knew about circles, squares, and rectangles now. Or he might even be able to sing a new song that his mother had taught him just that morning.

Whenever he began to sing, the family would lay down their spoons and forks, the food forgotten on their plates. And like the pure, sweet chimes that rang out at Christmas time, Louis's small voice would gently rise into the cottage room.

His expression intent, his thin body straining to help him remember the melody and the words, it was as if at those moments the music were a kind of *seeing* for Louis. And sometimes, near the end of his song, the family would join in with him, their voices supporting his as they swayed to the rhythm of Louis's music.

ɷ 3 ɷ

A WORLD OF TOUCH

Summer had come and gone, and now it was autumn. The Brailles' farmland had yielded enough corn, cabbages, onions, and beets to keep the table full of vegetables, and Monique's home-cooked bread, so warm and buttery under its crisp crust, helped to take away the chill from the first frosty mornings of September.

On weekdays, the village children left for school before the old town clock had sounded eight bongs. And by that hour, the Braille family had eaten breakfast, Simon René was working in the harness shop, and young Simon had fed the chickens, the cow, and the mare.

Nearly six months had passed since the accident with the awl. As Louis's other senses began to take over for the blankness in his eyes, his mind was quickly developing, too. Intelligent beyond his years, he wanted to share in the work of the family. He was quite aware that everyone else had chores to perform, yet he couldn't think of any job that he alone could do.

He always had to wait for someone to come and fetch him in the mornings, to help him dress and walk downstairs. And so often, he would have to sit for hours on the fireplace hearth while his legs seemed to ache for running or jumping, or even the scratchy feel of the haystacks that were piled high in his father's barn.

One morning as he lay curled up on his pallet, Louis listened carefully to the hushed stirrings of his family in the downstairs room. A toy dog, made of leather by his father, lay next to him on the straw. He touched the dog's nose, then traced his fingers up over the long, floppy ears. "Hear that noise?" he whispered to his toy. "That's my brother, Simon, going out the door. He'll be feeding the brown mare soon."

Seconds later, Louis poked the dog's stomach and rubbed his thumb over the stubby leather tail. "And hear *that*?" he said. "Well, Papa just filled the fireplace with logs and kindling."

Louis sat up in his strange, dark world and put on his shoes. Then he stood up. Although the dog was left behind on the straw matting, he kept talking to it as he slid along the wall with the palms of his hands. "Now, don't tell anyone," he whispered, "but I'm not going to wait for Mama or Marie or Catherine today. I'm going to go all the way downstairs by myself. No, you can't come with me. You're too little. But *I* know how to do it. It's easy, I won't fall. I learned how to count the steps."

And, somehow, he *had* learned. Carefully, he inched his way down the staircase. He counted as he went and listened for the scuff of his shoes on each stone step. When the sound changed—was more muffled—he was quite sure that he'd reached the downstairs room.

"Mama?" he called.

His parents were just coming in from the henhouse with the morning's eggs. "Louis!" Monique cried at the sight of him. "How did you ever walk downstairs?" She set the basket of eggs on the floor and was hurrying past the table when Simon René put out an arm and gently stopped her.

"Wait," he said, almost pleading. "Let the boy come to us. He only wants to show that he can look after himself."

Monique's clear blue eyes stared at her husband's face, then closed in a wince of pain. "I'll try," she said.

Haltingly, Louis moved away from the stairs. He struggled to remember where the roughhewn table was placed on the floor, how far the benches were

from the wall. But all that he could see was the blackness. For a moment, he felt as if he were standing on the edge of a huge hole—and that if he took one more step, he'd fall down and down and down. Then, in the next moment, it seemed as if he were shut up in a tiny, dark box where it was hard to breathe—and even harder to move.

His foot struck the leg of a stool. It tipped over onto the floor with a crash and then lay there on its rim, rocking back and forth.

Louis stopped, confused, and put out his hands. His mother stifled a moan and stepped toward him, but Simon René still held her arm. "It's all right, boy," he said soothingly. "It's just one of the stools. No harm done. Try and follow my voice, and come sit down for breakfast with me. There are ripe figs on the table this morning!"

Louis began again. Bit by bit, as his parents anxiously waited, he shuffled across the floor. After what seemed like hours instead of minutes, he bumped into the bench at the table, bent down to feel its familiar, worn top, and then held on while he climbed over and sat down.

"Good morning, Mama. Good morning, Papa," he said.

Simon René grinned and tousled his son's blond hair. Monique put a dish of hot cornmeal in front of Louis, while tears of relief and pride streamed down her face.

Slowly, Louis learned his way around the house. The tips of his fingers became like ten new "eyes." He could dig his hand into his father's pocket, pull out the coins, and announce each one without any hesitation. He could touch his mother's skirt and know which dress she wore by the texture of the cloth.

Once, when Marie and Catherine were leaving for town, Louis felt the string on Catherine's bonnet and said, "You're wearing Mama's new hat, aren't you?"

"Why, Louis!" Catherine said. "How did you ever know that?"

"It's easy," he told her. "I just looked with my fingers!"

Before October arrived, he was venturing out of doors by himself. His father had whittled a small cane for him, and he almost always took it with him and tapped it along the ground. He found that if he listened to the sounds of the cane or of his footsteps, he could get about with very few bumps or stumbles.

The sound waves of his walking told him things. If they hit against a tree trunk, a wagon, or a stool, they made a different sound than when he was just walking in open space. Sometimes he hummed or sang one of his songs, and then the waves were even stronger.

Unknowingly, he was discovering the secret of the bats that hung from the rafters of a neighbor's barn.

The bats moved in the dark, too, and were constantly making squeaking and clicking noises as they flew. When the sound waves from their noises bounced off objects, the bats were sufficiently warned to change their direction of flight.

Soon Louis had walked to the nearby well where his family drew their water. He traced his fingers over its rusted iron pipe and then turned toward the garden. Now and then he bent down and searched for the fall wildflowers that were hidden like tiny treasures in the grass. There was a tang of late autumn apples in the air, and he sensed that he'd found new ways of telling one season from another.

One day, he walked much farther—to the heavy old bridge that was down the hill from the village square. There he leaned against the high stone arch and listened happily to the roll and rumble of life around him. The tread of hoofbeats across the bridge seemed like the drumming in his own temples. Only a few weeks passed before he could tell the clippity-clop of a horse from the slow plod of a team of oxen, or could judge by the scraping of wheels whether a cart, a wheelbarrow, or a full-sized wagon was traveling by.

The villagers grew used to seeing him there on the bridge. "*Bonjour,* Louis! How are you?" they'd shout, and he'd wave and smile and call out their names. The sounds of their voices became as familiar to him as the touch of the brown mare at home or of the cool stone walls of the houses on his street. He seldom missed naming a friend, and he generally knew a city voice from the slower twang of country speech.

But, sometimes, he heard things that made him feel helpless and very sad. "Poor child!" people would whisper about him. "What a pity! What a waste!"

Wasn't he any good any more, he'd wonder. Was he like the colt that had been shot over on Moulin Street because it broke its leg and couldn't be useful?

Several nights before Christmas, when the cottage was filled with the heavy smell of fruitcake and scented pomander balls, Louis crouched on the staircase and overheard even his parents talking about the blind. "I've been told such terrible stories," his mother said, "about blind people in places like Paris. It's said that unless they're rich, they have to beg in the streets and wander about like animals. And it's said that some of them are sold to organ grinders and are forced to wear bells at their necks. Is that true, Simon? Are people really so cruel?"

"You mustn't worry," his father answered. "Louis will always be safe."

His mother's voice was trembling. "I still remember the day he was born. He was so little, so thin and red, and we weren't even sure that he would live. And remember, Simon, all the plans you had for him—that he would grow up to be a fine professor someday?"

"Let's not talk about that now," his father said. "Perhaps he can't go to school or learn a trade, but he will never have to beg. We'll save our money. We'll make sure that he's always cared for."

Louis crept back upstairs into the garret. But he didn't want to be just "cared for." Why couldn't he *do* something when he grew up? Why couldn't a blind boy be a real person, too? Hadn't his father always said that he would study books and someday be a learned man?

Louis felt tears stinging in the eyes that were useless and couldn't see. His father never talked about books anymore.

As the days passed, he tried much harder to be like the other boys. He would join in their games when they let him and lurch along after them. He'd hold their school books and carry their mittens and mufflers, and they thought he was nice and helpful and a bit odd. But he was just too *slow* for all their energy and impatience, and soon they'd run off without always realizing that he was left behind.

Then he was alone again in the darkness. A feeling of hunger began to gnaw within him—a hunger to take part and to belong. He'd press his fingers to his eyes and try to touch the blackness. Often, at night, he would dream with a dimming memory of sunlight and moonlight and candlelight and beautiful white flashes in the sky.

4

THE TRAMP OF BOOTS

Louis was growing taller. His blond curls had faded to the color of straw, and his eager, boyish face had narrowed. On his fifth birthday, he carried a new, much sturdier cane that his father had whittled for him, and he stood as straight as he could against a tree trunk in the courtyard to be measured for another "growing notch" in the bark.

"Papa," Louis shouted that morning. "When will I be as big as you are?"

Simon René looked down at the path of knife cuttings on the tree trunk. The three lowest marks had been put there when Louis could still see. "Why, I bet you're going to be bigger than I am someday!" Simon René had said.

In that early January, Louis often came back to

the marking tree and rubbed his fingers over the gnarled bark until he could feel the edges of the notch. Then he would walk up Touarte Street—his homemade cane tapping, tapping, tapping over the icy stones.

Sometimes a door would open along the winding street, and he would be invited into a steamy kitchen for a cup of hot, spicy onion soup or a freshly baked tart that was filled with sweet jelly.

The friendliness of housewives and farmers helped to make up for the playmates he seldom had. Neighbors felt sorry for the little blind boy who was, they thought, doomed to spend the rest of his life as a sad and useless burden. Hearts went out to Louis, but he was not given much hope—for it seemed certain that he would have nothing to contribute to his family or to the town.

Although shelters for the blind were built as early as the fourth century, and although medieval convents and monasteries usually had an almhouse for unfortunate people, the blind had stumbled through history on a lonely and terrifying road. Many had been locked away in mental institutions, or used as freak attractions, or simply left to wander in the streets. The world of instruction and learning—of books and schools, of factories and apprentice shops —had been shut off from them. In fact, to be blind meant to be helpless and unschooled and forever dependent on someone else.

In one period of Roman history, groups of blind beggars were ruled over by leaders who could see. These starving, shabby blind people were trained to whine and moan, and felt the lash of a whip if they didn't make enough pitiful cries. Then they were thrown out into the streets to beg for money that only fattened the stomach of a leader or perhaps bought him lodging for a night.

Compared to such brutality, little Louis was growing up in Coupvray surrounded with overwhelming kindness. And yet, in that winter of 1814, he, too, was about to taste deeper loneliness and even cruelty. The tragedy of his own life would be matched by a great tragedy for his country, as the Emperor Napoleon's Grand French Army failed in its attempts to conquer Russia and was itself conquered in a bloody and tumultuous war. . . .

The wind blew a few slivers of hay through the air as the Braille family waited in the raw and wintry square. Only an hour before, the village drum had begun to throb and rattle through the streets and fields of Coupvray, and the townspeople had put aside their work and hurried to meet together in the center square.

"Something must be wrong," they'd speculated among themselves. "The drum brings nothing but war news these days."

In the cottage, Monique had thrown a heavy wool

shawl around her shoulders before lifting the iron soup pot from its hook above the hearth. "We'll have to leave you at home for a little while," she'd told Louis. "I don't want our dinner to burn, so I'm putting the soup pot in the basin. Be very careful not to touch it."

"Oh, Mama," Louis had begged. "Please let me go, too!"

Monique had hesitated. The boy was past five now and able to use his cane with ease—but he might be jostled about by the crowds, and he might fall and hurt himself. But then she remembered how Simon René always told her not to treat their son as if he were sick. "Well," she'd said softly. "If you promise to stay close to us."

So Louis had been bundled into his winter clothes as the Brailles hastily prepared to leave the house. Now the family stood shivering in the cold morning air while the mayor climbed onto a wooden platform and asked for everyone's attention.

"This January was to be a time of hopeful planning for our village," the mayor finally said. "But today the news is not good. You all know that Napoleon's Grand French Army was defeated at the river Rhine. And just this morning the Emperor has sent word that he needs more help if he is still to win the war. Special messengers brought me the list of provisions that are to come from Coupvray."

Unrolling a long piece of parchment, the mayor

began to call out the requests for money and sup-
plies. Louis did not really understand what was
happening, but he was frightened by the sounds of
anger and shock that sprang through the crowd.

"One hundred and thirty-two bushels of oats," the
mayor was wearily calling, "1,200 bushels of hay,
706 loaves of bread, 150 cows, 73 horses. . . ." On
and on went the demands.

"What is it, Papa? What does that mean?" Louis
pleaded as he pulled on his father's arm. But it was
impossible for one small voice to be heard above so
much noise.

On the way home, Marie took Louis's hand while
Simon René tried to comfort his wife. "I think that
the tax we'll have to pay to the army comes to 320
francs," Simon René said. "But no matter how hard
we've been saving for Louis's future, we can begin
again when the war is over. And with the house and
the shop, the boy will always have a place of his
own after we're gone."

Louis reached up to touch his sister's hair. "How
long does war last?" he asked.

"I—I don't know, Louis," Marie said. "Even Papa
can't say for sure."

"It makes me feel afraid," Louis whispered.

Several days later, when the brown mare and the
cow were taken from his father's barn, Louis knew
for himself that war meant something more than
feeling afraid. It meant being sad, too—the way he

felt sometimes when he thought of never again seeing a star or the look of his mother's face.

He had wanted to act like a man that day at the
barn, but when he'd laid his cane on the ground and
had patted the mare's smooth belly for the last time,
the sobs burst up from his throat, and he cried to his
father, "Why, Papa? Why?"

Simon René had done his best to explain about the
battered and spent French troops. But Louis just
kept shaking his head back and forth, as if there
could be no answer to stop his tears. "The mare and
the cow belong to us!" he'd sobbed. "They're ours!"

"We must try and be brave," Simon René had said.

As the winter lengthened, the war was to have
still another meaning for Louis. The fear and sadness
became bewilderment, too—for so many changes
had come to Coupvray. The animals, food, and
money were in short supply, and even the weekly
market day was canceled because of empty cup-
boards and barns. A strange kind of quiet seemed
to smother the land, and Louis missed the smells
and sounds that once had guided him through the
streets.

No longer did the buttery smell of cookies thicken
the air by the bakery on a Wednesday morning.
There was no hammering in the yard where the
carpenter lived, no thunder of wheels across the
bridge—and where were the friendly voices that
used to call to him every day?

He still walked to the frozen brook or to the washhouse or up into the square. But now he might make
a wrong turn and wander helplessly until a house-
wife could manage to set him straight.

"Am I near the Cardiers' house?" he would ask
someone near. "I don't hear the geese behind the
gate."

"Over on the other side of the road," a villager
would answer, turning him this way or that. "The
geese were taken away last night. I don't know what
is to become of us all."

At home, only an occasional customer stopped to
leave an order at the harness shop. Hides of leather
hung uncut on the wall, and boxes of rivets waited
unopened on the bench. Louis could tell by the
quick touch of his fingers that very few reins or
straps had been sold since the winter—and the war
—had come to town.

Sometimes he would sit on the stone floor of the
shop, just as he'd done in much happier days. Pulling a small bunch of straw from his pocket and
placing several strands in front of him on the floor,
he would play the game that Catherine had taught
him. He had learned to build letters from the straw,
and often he pretended that he was making a book
and could read all the words on every page. Lightly,
he would trace the shape of a straw "L" with the
tip of his thumb. "*My* name begins with L," he

would say aloud, although there was no one to hear him. *"Louis Braille."*

When the spring came, Napoleon was in full retreat toward Paris. Six nations had squashed the attack on Russia, and suddenly there were enemy troops in Coupvray. One after another they came—Russian grenadiers, Bavarian infantry, Prussians, Russian cuirassiers—and now the town was stripped almost bare.

The Brailles' cottage shook with the beating of gunstocks on the door. Soldiers pushed into the downstairs room, looking for money and food. Monique had to cook for them, and they stamped their boots on the floor and yelled for wine and bread.

"Why are they here? What are they doing?" Louis had kept asking at first. How he'd longed to rip a hole in the darkness that held him so that he could actually *see* for himself.

But even the soldiers couldn't entirely change the habits of Coupvray. The town council still met that year to set the date for grape harvesting, just as they had done when Louis's grandfather had opened the shop at the foot of Touarte Street.

And on the evening before harvesting, the villagers still congregated in the square to sing the same songs and dance the same dances that always had been part of celebrating the grapes. However mournful voices may have sounded this season or however listlessly feet may have trod on the cobblestones, the war could not destroy this link with the past.

The next morning, Simon René took his family out into the sun-drenched vineyards. Although thoughts of his blind son and of empty barns were never far from his mind, the harness maker looked gratefully at the rows of rich and plentiful grapes. "At least God has not truly abandoned us," he whispered to himself. Then he turned to Louis and placed a faded wicker basket in the boy's arms. "You may be the one to pluck the very first fruit," Simon René said to his youngest son. "And be sure not to eat as much as you did last harvest! Remember how your mother had to put you to bed?"

Louis nodded and felt proud of this new responsibility that his father had given him. Walking stiffly, his head tilted to one side, he began the procession down the nearest row of vines. His fingers easily probed into the green leaves and stems, and soon the bottom of his basket was filled with plump and juicy grapes.

All day long, the family worked in the warm vineyards. Catherine moved in front of Louis to keep watch for any holes that might trip the boy, and she entertained him with a story about the castle of the princes of Rohan, which rose from a hill outside town.

"It must be wonderful to be a prince," Louis said. "Are they very smart?"

"I suppose they do learn about many things," Catherine answered.

"Do they go to school the way most children do?"

"Well—I—I suppose they do."

Louis stopped and rubbed his forehead. The sun suddenly felt so hot, and his eyes were aching as he remembered the shouts of the neighbor boys who left for school below his window. "Do you think there are any blind princes, Catherine?" he asked then.

His sister dropped her basket and spun around. Pulling Louis into her arms, she said, "You're as fine as *any* prince to me, Louis."

That evening, the villagers gathered in the square to discuss a new plan for sharing the few remaining work horses, oxen, and wagons that had not been taken by the war. Louis tried to listen to the talk, but then he leaned back against his mother's skirts, and the voices buzzed faintly in his ears.

"Come," Monique said, after one glance at her child's drawn and sleepy face. "We'll go home. You've done too much today."

Together, Louis and his mother walked slowly down the road toward the cottage. The night air was fragrant with the smell of clover, and crickets snapped lustily in the grass. But as he climbed the three familiar steps to his house, Louis found the oak door ajar and heard the harsh, throaty laughter that meant soldiers were once again inside.

"Don't be frightened," his mother told him. "Perhaps they won't stay long."

Standing in the doorway, Louis could smell the tobacco and wine, and he felt the crumbling dirt under his shoes that heavy boots had tramped in from the fields.

"Ah—what's this?" a loud voice called in slurred French. "A *blind* one? Well, I hope you brought someone with you that can make us dinner."

Louis swayed dizzily in exhaustion. Were these *French* soldiers, he wondered. But the French troops had come through Coupvray last spring. Could they be what his brother Simon called "deserters," men who'd run away from the army?

"Why don't you go upstairs and rest, Louis," he heard his mother say.

Obediently, he started toward the stairs. But then he stopped. If his father and brother had been there, would they leave just because they felt afraid? The darkness seemed to wrap itself around him, but he turned back and moved cautiously toward the table.

Suddenly, another voice jeered, "There are already enough blind beggars from this bloody war. If you let this one loose on the streets of Paris, he'd starve in a week. Better to put him in a pen and feed him like the pigs!"

A stool scraped across the floor, and Louis felt two

thumps near his feet. "There, boy!" Someone laughed. "Let's see if you're good for anything. Clean my boots!"

Laughter and belching filled the room. Still, Louis heard the swish of his mother's skirts as she sped around the table and commanded shakily, "Leave him alone!"

But he shook his head and crouched down to the floor. Sweeping his hands out in circles until he could feel the boots, he carefully picked them up by their dusty leather tops. "That's all right, Mama," he said in a small, strained voice. "I can clean the boots very well. I can do a lot of things."

Then he raised his face toward the bittersweet smell of wine and smoke, and as all the sadness, fear, and bewilderment flooded through him, he found the courage to add, *"You'll see."*

✆ 5 ✆

LESSONS FROM A FRIEND

The old church in the village had been a comfort in the long and miserable months of the war. Women with their heads wrapped in scarves would slip softly down the pews and kneel to pray in silence beneath the window. Men who roamed the streets with no work to do would come to sit by the altar, their strained faces slowly growing calm. On Sundays, early morning Mass was given by the Abbé Pillon. And afterwards, as the wide church doors swung open for the villagers, it seemed that the marching of soldiers was only distant thunder on the streets.

But then Father Pillon died, and the church was somehow empty even when the people came to make it full. Down the street, the door to the presbytery was locked since there was no one to live in it anymore. And suddenly, the war seemed louder and stronger, and the villagers grew bitter and more pale.

Sometimes Monique would drop a string of rosary beads into her young son's pocket when he asked to leave the house. Remembering the sound of hymns on Sunday mornings, Louis would choose to climb the hill toward the presbytery and the old stone church. These days, however, he only heard the plaintive calls of pigeons that gathered on the roofs.

"The birds are hungry, too," Monique told her husband. "I know that Louis has been feeding them cornmeal, and although we have hardly a bite to spare, I cannot bring myself to make him stop."

"Let him be," Simon René answered. "For once, he is able to give help—instead of always to need it. For that I would gladly eat only twice a week myself."

In February, a new pastor was sent to the war-stricken village. Father Jacques Palluy had come from a monastery to reopen the vacant church in Coupvray. Walking among the soldiers who lounged in the streets, his black robes billowing out against their drab, mud-spattered uniforms, the Abbé paid a visit to each family in his parish.

"He is a fine man," Simon René said after Father Palluy had called at the cottage on Touarte Street.

"I liked him, too, Papa!" Louis said.

"I could tell so by your face. It is said in town that the Abbé is quite learned and was once a Benedictine monk. He seemed very pleased, Louis, when you showed him your letters made from straw."

Louis could soon mark a new sound on the steep, winding streets of the village. A certain swish and sweep of heavy cotton meant that the Abbé was walking nearby, and then the deep voice would exclaim, "Will you keep me company again, Louis? It is such a blessing when you tell me the names of the families that I shall be visiting today!"

It was Father Palluy who was there on the morning the soldiers took Louis's cane. A bored and sullen band of grenadiers had watched the young blind boy edge past them, carrying a handful of cornmeal up toward the frozen churchyard. "You're lugging too many things, boy," snickered one of the men. "Here, let me lighten your load!"

Grabbing the cane from Louis's hand, the soldier lifted it high into the air. Louis could only utter a small, strangled cry as he turned helplessly on the street. "Please, monsieur," he said. "Don't throw it away! I won't be able to find my way home without it!"

"Oh, now!" The soldier laughed. "Why is that? It's only a wooden stick, isn't it—a simple wooden stick that you might find anywhere? You'll just have to go into the fields and *look* for another!"

By this time, the other soldiers had seen a chance

for sport, and the cane was passed from one pair of hands to the next. Their voices shouted gleefully, "It's over here, boy! Over here! *No*, it's over there!"

But as two of the grenadiers hung the cane on a water trough, Father Palluy rushed from the presbytery door. "What is going on?" he demanded. "Give that cane back to the boy at once! What sort of men are you to make fun of a blind child?"

Grumbling, the soldiers moved away down the hill. The Abbé retrieved the cane from the handle of the trough and placed it gently in Louis's arms. "Come," Father Palluy said. "We'll go into my study for a while."

Louis had never been behind the presbytery doors. In the Abbé's study, he touched the chairs and the desk and the tall candle in its pewter base. Then he found the bookshelves on the wall.

Father Palluy watched quietly as Louis rubbed his fingers over the rows and rows of books. Reaching above him as far as he could, Louis felt the edges of the leather bindings. Stretching his arms out on either side, his fingertips passed over the thick volumes on a lower shelf. "So many," he said softly. "I never knew there were so many books."

"Would you like to hold one, Louis?" Father Palluy asked.

The soldiers who had taken his cane were suddenly forgotten. "Oh, yes—if I might. I'll be very careful!"

The Abbé reached for a book that lay on top of the desk. "This is one of my Bibles," he said. "Sit down over here, Louis. Now, then, you will be surprised at how thin the pages are—like the wings of a dragonfly."

Louis opened the cover and turned several pages. "I wish that I could see the words," he said.

Father Palluy looked down at the boy's slender fingers. "You know," the priest said, "I would think that it is possible to enjoy a great many things, even if you can't see them. I heard about a blind man who lived in England some years ago. His name was John Metcalf—and, once, he walked two hundred miles to London by himself, just because he wanted to visit Windsor Castle on the way."

Louis lifted his head. "Really? And he was *blind?* What else did he do?"

"Well, he could swim like a fish. And he had ninety great-grandchildren by the time he was ninety-three!"

Louis laughed and leaned forward eagerly in the chair. How he loved a story! "Tell me more, Father!" he said. "Tell me how *I* can learn to swim!"

When Louis left the presbytery that day, he was asked to come again. The Abbé bid him good-bye at the door, and he started his journey home along the cobblestoned street. But halfway down the hill, he turned to wave his cane in the air. "*Au revoir,*

Father!" he called. "I thank you for letting me touch your books! I thank you for the good story!"

The Abbé gave a wave, too, and then realized that Louis would not be able to see it. "Thank you for your company, Louis!" he called back. "We will meet again soon for more stories. *Au revoir,* my little friend!"

The pieces of straw that Louis kept in the garret were rarely used for letter-making now. The stories from Father Palluy's books were remembered and retold after suppers in the cottage, and Louis would think them all over again when he'd gone upstairs to bed.

Two or three times a week, he tapped his way up to the presbytery to spend an hour or so with the priest. The Bible characters became nearly real to him, and he had learned also some simple history and astronomy, of how men lived differently in places far from Coupvray, of what it meant to be brave or honest or wise.

With the warmer weather, he and the Abbé often sat in the garden of the presbytery under flowering trees. The pigeons came to shuffle at Louis's feet while his head seemed to whirl with delight at the stories he would hear.

He felt that it was possible to tell any secret at all to Father Palluy. He talked about the soldiers who laughed at him and of the times he was afraid. He told of the dreams he had at night, where he could see like everyone else—and then of how he'd wake in the morning and try to open his eyes, only to find that they *were* open and that the darkness was there as before.

On his seventh birthday, Father Palluy gave him a book of French songs that had been written for the voice and the lute. The Abbé sang as many of the songs as he knew, and Louis learned them by ear—and by heart. It was the first book that he had ever owned, and he kept it under the knitted blanket on his pallet. Often, if the family were busy with their chores, he would open the deerskin cover and touch the pages with tender care.

Whenever Catherine, who was married now, came to see him, he would lead her upstairs by the hand and ask her to sing him some of the songs. "Aren't they lovely, Louis!" she would say. "Do you remember how we all used to sing around the table when you were a very little boy?"

The thought of the book stayed with him when he walked the streets of town. And it must have been the book that spurred him on past his usual boundaries, to set out on an adventure of his own.

Carrying the book under his jacket, to hide it from the soldiers, he found the path that led up to the schoolhouse where the other children went each day. The bump of stones under his cane helped to give him his bearings, but he was fearful of this new place where his fingers touched only tree bark and bushes and where the loudest sounds were from blackbirds who couldn't possibly tell him the way.

Leaning his head to one side, he kept listening for the crunch of stones on the path, and he followed its dips and turns until he heard the chanting of voices up ahead. Then his steps grew more wary, and as a thickening cushion of air told him that he might be approaching a wall, he abruptly came to a stop.

With one arm outstretched, he felt the sharp corner of a windowsill and hastily drew back. *Oh, they mustn't find me here!* he thought. *I don't belong!* But he leaned forward again to skim his fingers over the rough stone and to listen to the murmur of voices on the other side of the wall.

What would it be like, he wondered, if he were a boy who could see? He would run all through the village, wouldn't he, and he'd watch for the moon to hang like one of his mother's crescent cookies in the evening sky. He'd stare for hours at the faces of everyone he knew, and he'd know what his sister Marie meant when she said that the hen's feathers were "as white as the snow."

But, most of all, he would go to school. He would write so many papers that Monsieur Becheret, the teacher, would have to use up twenty pencils just to correct them. And he'd read so many books that a library would have to be built in Coupvray, almost as big as the Bibliothèque Nationale that Father Palluy told him was in the city of Paris, full of books that had been given by kings.

A sudden commotion behind the wall made Louis stumble away in search of the path. At the first scattering of a few stones under his shoes, he hurried in his stilted fashion along the gravel, not daring to linger for another moment, hoping that he wouldn't be seen if the school doors should open for recess in the yard.

The wind pushed at his neck, and he slid the songbook out from under the bottom of his jacket. But it was not long before he knew that something was wrong. Tucking his cane and the book under one arm, he bent down to touch the pathway, finding that the stones were embedded in hard, smooth earth—not lying loose as they were when he'd made the trip up, just a short time ago.

He walked on gingerly, as if the ground might crack open and swallow him up. Soon, the stones had disappeared completely, and he knew that it was too late to retrace his steps. He must have taken the wrong path in his haste to flee from the school. There was nowhere to go now, no landmarks to guide him home. A word fluttered against his thoughts like the baby duckling that he'd once cupped in his hands during a storm—lost, lost, lost!

His cane grazed across a tree trunk, and he sat

down, telling himself that he shouldn't be afraid because the darkness was the same for him wherever he was. He waited there for more than an hour, poised for the slightest signal or clue. Finally, he heard the faint sound of laughter and pulled himself to his feet. "Help!" he called. "Over here! Help!"— but his voice faded into the distance, and no one answered his calls.

Raindrops began to spatter on the leaves above his head, and he carefully tucked the songbook back inside his jacket. He thought of trying to walk wherever his feet would lead him, in the hopes of finding someone who would take him back to town.

But if there were streams of water nearby or traps set for animals, or if he walked in just the opposite direction from Coupvray— No, he felt sure that his mother and father would tell him to stay by the tree. In fact, he could almost hear their voices saying, "Don't be afraid, Louis! We shall be coming to take you home."

Still, he *was* a little afraid. Because if no one should ever find him, what would happen to him, what would he do? Lying down on the ground, he buried his face in his arms. The rain was falling more heavily now, but he whispered fiercely, "They'll come. I know they'll come."

Yet it was hours later, long after midnight, before a group of men from the village hurried with torches into the field where Louis had strayed. Simon René and the Abbé Palluy had led the group all through that night, and then at last, in the orange glow from the torches, was the welcome sight of a small boy lying with wide, blank eyes and rain-soaked clothes.

Simon René threw himself to the ground, clutching his son in his arms. "Oh, Louis," he said, his voice cracking. "What happened? Where have you been?"

"You did come, Papa! You did! I took the wrong path, and I wasn't sure how to get back."

"We've been searching for hours," his father said. "The Abbé is with me, and so are many others. But what path, Louis? What were you doing out here?"

"I walked to school, Papa."

"To *school?* What for?"

The Abbé Palluy stooped down beside the tree. "I should have known, Simon. The boy speaks so often of school."

Louis could no longer keep back his tears. "I walked along the outside, that's all. I didn't make any noise, and I only stayed for a little while. But I wonder why I couldn't just *listen* in school, Papa— the way I listen to Father Palluy's stories. Why do they keep me out? Why must it be so terrible to be blind?"

Simon René turned to the Abbé for help. And as Father Palluy looked off into the darkness of the night, where the schoolhouse waited above the hill, he was reminded of other men throughout history who had tried to give comfort to the blind—Basil of

Caesarea, William the Conqueror, King John the Good, King Louis IX of France. The Abbé's eyes sought to pierce the darkness beyond the bright halos of flame that burned from the torches, but he could see nothing, just as Louis could not see. And yet all the boy had asked for was the chance to listen, in the room of a schoolhouse above the hill.

"Perhaps there is something I can do, Louis," Father Palluy said.

~~ 6 ~~

"I WANT TO READ!"

The neighbor boy whistled as he came up the street called Chemin des Buttes toward the Brailles' cottage. Louis waited outside, his cheeks rosy, his cane tapping impatiently against the stone steps. *"Bonjour,* Louis," the other boy said. "Are you ready?"

"I was awake before the blackbirds!" Louis laughed. "And wondering if you would ever come at all. Look—my father cut out a leather strap for the books that I might bring home today!"

Walking together as their families had planned, the two boys climbed the hill toward the upper village. At the schoolhouse, Louis was assigned a seat on the very first bench. Lovingly, he traced his fingers over the books on a table and touched the timeworn grooves on the desk tops, and he felt a kind of happiness that he'd never known before.

Monsieur Becheret had an extra reading primer for his new student. "But what benefit would there be in issuing such a book to a blind boy?" the teacher asked himself. Then, as he recalled how persuasive the Abbé Palluy had been about this unfortunate child, Antoine Becheret laid the primer in Louis's lap. "Your brother and sisters studied from this same book, Louis. They should enjoy reading it to you at home, don't you think?"

"*Oui*, monsieur!" Louis said. "I shall try very hard to learn the stories."

All through that morning and afternoon, Louis drank in every word of Monsieur Becheret's lessons. And when five o'clock arrived and the students were dismissed, it seemed as if he were leaving a magic land.

He did not need long to adjust to the routine of school—a day of lessons by the teacher, the next day given to recitation by the class—and soon he was finding new ways to substitute ears and fingers for sight. Neighbor children took turns reading homework pages to him, and by touching the jackets of his schoolmates as they played outside, he learned to call their names even in the midst of a large and noisy crowd.

Monsieur Becheret reported to the Abbé that his

newest pupil had a keen and utterly amazing mind. When asked to recite, Louis would remember the lessons of the week as if he had heard them only moments before. And often he would figure out arithmetic problems more quickly in his head than another child might do with two good eyes, a notebook, and a pen.

After several months, he was at the top of his class in achievement—a seven-year-old boy who couldn't read or write and who couldn't see!

The mayor and the town council made no fuss about Louis's going to school. Perhaps that was because the village authorities felt sorry for the harness maker's son and chose to ignore the teaching policy of the day. Or perhaps it was because after two troubled and dismal years, the enemy occupation was ending, and at last there was work to be done in Coupvray.

Louis heard the shouts of the Russian officers as grenadiers and infantrymen were called into formation at the village square. And he stood near the corner to listen to the familiar tramping of boots that shook the shutters on the housefronts. But this time, the sounds grew fainter and fainter as the soldiers moved on toward the next town of Meaux and then would be gone from there, too.

Villagers danced in the streets that morning, and school was let out for a holiday. Flocks of children mocked the departing soldiers by trudging up and down the cobblestones, shrieking, "Forward—march! One, two—one, two! Halt!"

And how quickly the months seemed to pass as soon as the soldiers were gone. Without the burden of war, Coupvray was again a fertile land tended by people who were used to a life that pulled at their muscles and toughened their minds. The rich soil sent up sprouts of vegetables, while cows, pigs, colts, and chickens were born and nurtured in the barns. Men in uniform no longer stole the crops or slaughtered the animals, and once more the children knew the taste of milk and buttered bread.

Handsome carts and wagons popped up everywhere in town, the clacking of their wheels like a lively song. The center square bustled again on market day as merchants and tradesmen set up their wares, and Simon René's harness shop was filling with orders for harnesses and repairs.

"Come outside, Louis!" Simon René said one evening. "There's a stranger standing by the barn!"

Louis hurried over the soft, sloping ground. Then his father took hold of his hand and guided it around two pointed ears that felt like velvet, and a mane that was smoother than a harness's newly made fringe. "Papa!" Louis shouted. "Is it a *mare?* Is she *ours?*"

"She is, indeed!" Simon René said. "The mayor

paid me for the three saddles, and I brought the mare home from a farm up at Meaux."

Now Louis would run into the barn after school and nuzzle the mare's head against his neck. Then he might hasten across the yard to the street and climb the steps to the harness shop door. Inside, he would dip his fingers into the brine water where the leather thongs were soaking so as not to shrink. The vats for the brine had been empty since the year before, and the water felt cool and silky to the touch.

His father would always ask, "Well, what did my son learn today in school?" and Louis might speak about the time of the Revolution or the way that pencils were made with graphite and clay. His mother would come to the door to give him a hot roll covered with cheese, and he began to think that there was nothing more wonderful than to be a boy of almost ten who went to school.

But such happy days were not to last. One winter afternoon, Father Palluy waited at the bend of the path near school, having told Monique and Simon René that, since he had encouraged Louis's studies, no one else should bear the responsibility of breaking the bad news.

The Abbé called to Louis from the pathway. "How are you?" Father Palluy asked. "May we walk together into town?"

"Of course, Father!" Louis said. "It's very cold,

isn't it? I am going to thaw out my feet for an hour in front of the hearth!"

"*Oui,* very cold. But there is something that I came to tell you while we walk."

Louis had never heard such concern in the priest's voice. "Oh," he said. "Is it about me, Father?"

"*Oui*—it is. I have been speaking with the mayor, Louis. He informs me that Monsieur Becheret is to be sent away for a time, to be trained in a new method of teaching. And while the school is empty, most of the children will be taught over in the town of Lesches. Yesterday, I went to see the headmaster there, and although I explained how very well you've done in school, he—"

Louis had known for several moments just what the Abbé would say, but slowly and firmly he made himself pronounce the words. "In Lesches, they don't allow blind children to attend school, do they?"

"I am afraid not. So much of the world still has something to learn, Louis—that true light or darkness is found in the spirit and not in the eyes. But you and I will not despair. With the help of God, we will be shown the right way for you."

Louis walked woodenly along the path. "But why did God ever have to make me blind?" he asked.

Father Palluy struggled to find the words that he wanted. "I think God can help us," he answered at last, "with what happens here on earth. And I think

He may have a special mission, Louis, just waiting for someone like you."

Louis's school strap was hung from a high hook in his father's harness shop. Simon René covered it over with a bridle and kept his son busy winding thongs and learning to weave a fringe. Often, Louis sat quietly at the workbench with his book of French songs—only inches away from the awl that once had taken his sight.

Catherine came by to read to him, and his mother baked tiny iced cakes. And even the new calf seemed to understand his sorrow as she wobbled sweetly against him out in the yard.

And so the winter set in, with its coat of frost over the bleak, barren fields, until one evening Father Palluy paid another visit to the darkened cottage on Touarte Street. With a flickering candle held in her hand, Monique curtsied low before the priest and offered him a place at the table.

Father Palluy's eyes gleamed as brightly as the flame from the candlewick. "There is an answer!" he began. "I have found a school, an extraordinary school in the city of Paris. It's the work of a famous teacher named Valentin Haüy and is attended *only* by boys who are blind! Ah, my friends, just wait until you hear—the blind children there can play the piano and the violin. They learn a trade and make their own clothing and shoes. It's the first institution of its kind in the entire world!"

Louis came slowly from the hearth. "Music?" he said wonderingly. "The piano—and the violin?"

The Abbé reached across the table to put a hand on Simon René's shoulder, then turned to look directly at the boy. "And something far more wonderful, Louis." Father Palluy beamed. "The instructors at this school have learned a way of teaching the blind how to *read*."

Louis put out his hands to keep from falling. What was that sound, he asked himself, that seemed to burst over the room like a sudden pealing of bells? *Read?* Had Father Palluy truly said *read?* Yes, yes, yes! He had!

"The school may be expensive," the Abbé explained. "But Louis performed so well under Antoine Becheret that I think he would qualify for a scholarship. And there is someone I know of influence, a Monsieur d'Orvilliers, who might put in a good word with the director."

"Oh, Mama, Papa!" Louis shouted. "May I go? I want to learn to read!"

Monique shook her head as she turned from her husband to the priest. "Paris is too far," she said fearfully. "More than half a day's journey from Coupvray. Who will watch out for the boy? How can we send him so far from home?"

For Simon René, a spurt of memory came back from the past—from the day of Louis's birth. "This one shall be a professor!" he had proclaimed. Now, as he looked down at his son's glowing face, Simon René answered, "How can we not send him? He'll learn to *read!*"

That same week, a letter was dispatched to the National Institute for Blind Youth at No. 68 Rue St. Victor—Paris, France. On January 25, a meeting was held at the school, and an application was considered for one Louis Braille of Coupvray, age ten.

In due course, a return letter was sent by the school director, Dr. Sebastian Guillié. Louis Braille had been accepted, Dr. Guillié wrote. A scholarship had been awarded, and it was here stated that the young man should present himself for entrance on February 15 of the same year, 1819.

Louis had never been any distance from his family, but the thought of a school for blind boys left him no room for more than a twinge of fear. In the garret of the cottage, he held the treasured letter open against his cheek. The crisp paper was as smooth as an eggshell, but it really didn't matter if he couldn't see or feel the words. They were there— and they seemed to have spoken just to him.

7

ONLY A FEW BOOKS

Dr. Guillié took the bundle from Louis's arms and pushed it under the narrow dormitory bed. "We have no place for food that the mothers send up here. You'll have to keep it under your bed—and be sure to eat it before it spoils."

"*Oui*, Docteur," Louis said. His legs felt cramped in the tight trousers of his school uniform, but at least the jacket with the metal buttons was warm against his back.

"And now that you are dressed," Dr. Guillié said, "we shall go at once to Monsieur Dufau's geography class."

Louis let the director guide him swiftly along the chilly corridors. He listened to the throb and rattle of echoes overhead, and once when he touched the walls, his fingers slid away as if the surface were wet.

Then a door opened, and Dr. Guillié led him forward by the shoulder. "Excuse me, Monsieur Dufau, but a new boy has just arrived. His name is Louis Braille, and he is the youngest of our sixty students— only ten years old. I am confident that the class will make him welcome. Continue with your lecture, *s'il vous plaît.*"

With that, Louis felt the hand on his shoulder prodding him on until he was told that an empty seat was waiting and that he should sit down.

"Attention, class!" Monsieur Dufau said sharply. "As I explained, it was in 1808 that the Great Tower of the Temple was torn down in Paris. Its turret walls were nine feet thick and hid the king on the night before he died on the guillotine. But, today, if you were to go to the spot where the tower once stood, you would walk through a public garden with newly planted trees."

Louis tried to pay attention, but the stream of words seemed to roll themselves into a knot inside his chest. All that he could think of was the ride in the swaying stagecoach and the noises of the city, and then the crush of his father's coat against his own face as they'd hugged good-bye on the steps.

"Now mind your manners and study hard," his father had said. "And don't forget your prayers. The director will see that you attend Mass on Sundays— and, oh yes, there'll be someone to write letters home

for you. Your mother will be waiting for news as the
queen bee waits for the first spring flower!"

Louis had laughed and promised to be faithful
with his letters. Then his father had added quickly,
"Tell us if you need anything, son—more sweaters
or perhaps a thicker blanket. The building is a bit
damp, isn't it?"

Now, as Louis sat in a schoolroom where others
were said to share his darkness, he heard his name
called and jumped shakily to his feet.

"*Louis Braille,*" Monsieur Dufau said. "Was the
king alone on that fateful night before his death?"

Anxiously, Louis tried to remember the last half
hour of lecture. Hadn't he always known the answers
for Monsieur Becheret? But this time, on his first day
in Paris, he was unprepared. "I—I—I'm not sure," he
stammered.

"But I have *just said* that his wife and children
were also sheltered in the tower! You do have two
good *ears*, don't you? Let us hope, Louis Braille,
that your short memory is not an omen of what is
to come."

Louis's cheeks burned with embarrassment. "*Non,*
monsieur," he said softly.

A bell rang to signal the end of class, and Louis
sat uncertainly in his chair. Around him, he heard
the others hurrying away. What should he do?
Where should he go? Would there be stairs to climb?

Then someone leaned over him. "Monsieur Dufau

is very strict," said a boy's raspy voice. "Sometimes, if I fail a test, he locks me in a room by myself for the whole afternoon. Would you like to change to history class with me? I'm to be your guide for the day. My name is Jean d'Anjou."

Gratefully, Louis let the boy take his arm as they walked into the hall. "After a while, you'll be able to move about here by yourself," Jean told him. "I don't even have to count the steps anymore. And if you call out your name when you pass students in the corridors, they will soon know you."

"The school seems so big," Louis said.

"Oh, it's big enough—and they barely feed you enough to keep you alive. But it's better than being at home. My mother couldn't wait to get rid of me."

"But she must miss you very much now," Louis said. He thought of being at home in Coupvray, warmed by a fire in the hearth, and of the clatter of the dishes as his mother set the table for supper. Did his own parents know about children being locked up in rooms at the school or maybe not having much of anything to eat? No, they couldn't have known, or they never would have let him stay in such a place. *Papa! Papa! Come back!* he wanted to shout.

That night, when the classes were over, beans and porridge were served in the drafty dining hall. Afterwards, with Jean at his side, Louis was guided upstairs to the dormitory and helped to find his bed.

"Well, *bonsoir,* Louis," Jean told him. "I'll come and fetch you in the morning."

Then Jean was gone, and Louis was left to manage on his own. Awkwardly, he shuffled back and forth across the dormitory, counting eighteen steps between the door and the iron foot rail on his bed. Other boys brushed past him, joking among themselves, and finally he undressed, leaving his uniform neatly folded over a table that was set against the wall.

Only moments later, another bell rang and the room was instantly hushed. Quivering with fear and loneliness and cold, Louis crawled under the thin, fraying cover on the bed. "Eighteen steps. Eighteen. Eighteen," he kept saying to himself. "I mustn't forget."

"Are you Louis Braille?" came a sudden whisper from the next cot.

"Oui," Louis said, his teeth chattering.

"I'm Gabriel Gauthier. They told me that you would be coming. You don't live in Paris, do you? You have a different accent."

"Non. I'm from Coupvray. It's in the country. It's —very nice there."

"I was homesick for a while at school," Gabriel said. "But I'm not anymore. One gets over it, you know."

Louis swallowed. "I hope so," he whispered back.

Then, pushing himself up against the headboard, he asked eagerly, "Have you learned to read any books?"

"Not yet. But the teachers say I'll soon be given a try at one of the books."

Louis wanted the friendly voice from the next bed to never, never stop. "Gabriel," he said. "I just thought of something! I have a package of chicken and cookies that my mother sent. It's right under my bed! Are you hungry?"

"Well, we're not supposed to eat after the final night bell. But the porridge was so lumpy at dinner that I'd surely love a taste of chicken!"

"I'll get it!" Louis said. He slipped out of the covers and bent down on the floor until his arm could reach under the metal bedsprings. But the space was empty. Perplexed, he pushed himself farther under the bed. Rubbing his hands up and down on the cold wooden floor, his fingers gritty with dust, he searched and searched for the package. But there was no package to be found.

"Gabriel," he said when he'd climbed slowly back onto the blanket. "My food isn't here anymore. It's disappeared."

"Oh, Louis, I'm so sorry! Sometimes the older boys come and steal from a new student. They took my father's war medal that he let me keep."

"But, *why?* Why would they do such a thing?" Louis asked.

"I don't know, Louis. That's just the way it is here."

How often, in that beginning week, Louis was to think of Gabriel's words—*That's just the way it is here*—for as he tried to unravel the maze of halls, corners, and stairs in the Institute, he was met with taunts about his country accent and jeers from the older students about his being the "baby Braille." Tearfully, he kept bumping into the cold, clammy walls in the corridors, and the teachers that he met hardly took time to say hello.

There were some moments when he forgot that he was now more miserable than he'd ever been before in his life. In the slipper shop, he was fascinated with the touch of the leather strips that, piece by piece, were made into shoes by the students. The smooth leather under his fingers was like the feel of the harness shop and of home. And in the music room, he strummed a strange instrument called a harp. The deep, rolling sounds that surged forth were more beautiful to him than the chords from the organ that he used to hear in church.

But if he dared to speak his mind, Louis was promptly put in his place. When he asked the music teacher about learning to play the harp, he was rapped on the knuckles with a ruler and told never to touch the instrument again—that it was meant only for second-year students. And when he spoke to Monsieur Dufau about finding the library of books, the geography teacher snapped, "Why must you be so impatient? Aren't you the same boy who asked to have a book merely two days ago? Books, books, books! There are more important things to learn about here!"

On the first Sunday that Louis spent at the Institute, he was taken to church along with a group of other boys. Ordered into a single file, the students placed their left hands around a thick rope that was passed among them. Then, picking up the front end of the rope, an instructor called out, "*Alors!* Let us go!"

In uniform, weaving in line like a big blue caterpillar along the Paris streets, the students were led toward the church of St. Nicholas des Chardonnerets. Windows were raised on the houses that leaned in crooked rows over the sidewalk, and people parted their curtains to look down and say, "There go the blind boys to Mass!"

Louis liked to be out in the air. The stale smell of the Institute was so heavy, and at last he felt that he could breathe deeply again. Inside the church, he knelt to say his prayers and then was hurried down an aisle into the pews. The hollow sounds of his footsteps told him that the building was large, and he wondered what the Abbé Palluy would think of the choir that was singing hymns in such perfect pitch.

By his second week at school, Louis found that
Jean d'Anjou was allowed to take short walks in the
neighborhood without a guide, and he asked if he
might go along. Dr. Guillié finally agreed after Louis
recited almost all the facts from the past week of
history lectures, and on a late afternoon the two boys
set off for a bakery several blocks away.

"Jean," Louis said when the Institute seemed
safely behind. "Have *you* read any of the books for
the blind?"

"Of course. I've read them all. A long time ago."

Louis nearly stumbled on the pavement. "You've
read them *all?* Every book in the school library?"

"Louis, you wouldn't really call a room with three
books and a few pamphlets a *library*, would you?"

"But—I thought—" Louis didn't finish his sentence.
The lump that clogged his throat was stinging, and
he just couldn't bear to have Jean laugh at him. Only
three books—only *three?* But he'd hoped, he'd
dreamed—he'd imagined a whole roomful of
books. . . .

Jean squeezed his arm. "Maybe you thought there
was a real library, eh?"

"What are they like?" Louis asked stiffly. "What
sort of books are they?"

"Oh, they're filled with big, bumpy letters, raised
off the paper for touching. It can take more than a
page just to hold eight or ten words. With books like

those, there will never be any *library* for the blind."

"But without enough books," Louis said, "how can we ever really learn?"

"I don't want any more of the embossed-letter books," Jean answered. "You try to read all those zigzagging letters, and you forget the beginning of a sentence before you can even figure out the end of it. Valentin Haüy, the man who founded the school, paid a lot of money to have the books printed with a special type, and maybe he's disappointed, too. But the teachers won't talk about Monsieur Haüy. He's some kind of mystery at school. Anyway, I suppose the raised letters are easier than the ones that used to be made from pinpoints. Ouch! How that must have hurt the fingers!"

Louis felt tears of disappointment streaking down his cheeks. But he knew that Jean would not be able to see him cry. "At home," he mumbled, "our pastor told me that students from the Institute once read their books before the king and queen."

"We've always been a freak attraction, haven't we?" Jean said. "Today the reading is only a show for society ladies who make tours through the school. Ah well, what else can they do for us blind boys? Don't feel too bad, Louis, we're at the bakery. I can just taste the cookies and the blueberry tarts!"

Under a faint sound of chimes, Louis was met by the spicy smell of fresh pastry. Wiping his face, he gave Jean the few francs that were in his pocket. "You choose something for me," he said. "I'm not very hungry."

"Not hungry!" exclaimed a woman's cheerful voice. "But we can't have that. You'll be doing my bakery an injustice! How would it please you young gentlemen if I picked out two of my fattest and creamiest éclairs?"

"Mmmmmm!" Jean said. "How does that sound to you, Louis?"

"Fine," Louis said, moving closer to the counter. A certain lilt to the woman's voice reminded him of a neighbor who lived near the marketplace in Coupvray. Wouldn't it be nice, he thought, if he didn't have to go back to the Institute right now and if he could just stay in a warm corner of the bakery, helping the store woman to take her cookies and cakes from the oven.

But by the time he had followed Jean's footsteps out of the store, the éclairs wrapped snugly in two paper bags, he was feeling a bit better about returning to the harshness of school. *Well,* he began thinking, *if there are only a few books for blind boys, I shall learn to read them. And next I'll try all the pamphlets. And by then, the school might have a new way of teaching us how to read. Why, someday, there could be thousands of books for the blind!*

Suddenly, he heard a burst of laughter and cackling, and felt someone snatch the pastry bag

from his hand. "Wait!" he cried at the swish of clothing and the scratching of many pairs of shoes. Ahead
of him, Jean was shouting, "Give that back! Who are
you? *Allez-vous-en!* Give it back! It's mine!"

Louis flapped the air with his cane as a band of
dirty and poorly dressed boys danced in circles on
the street. "Bullies!" Jean screamed. Then something
wet and sticky slapped against Louis's leg. Cringing
against the front of a building, he felt another lump,
and then another, hit him on the side.

"Run, Louis!" Jean screamed at him. "They're
throwing horse manure at us! Horse manure! Oh, it's
all over me! Take my hand! Try not to fall!"

Sobbing, Louis staggered down the street, the
yells of "Ugly eyes! Ugly eyes!" beating against his
ears. He held onto Jean's coattails all the way back
to the Institute, and climbed the steps with his lungs
straining and heaving for air.

The following afternoon, he crept out of the main
door of the school unnoticed. Feeling his way along
the walls of buildings, fearing that every sound on
the street meant that the bullies would jump out at
him again, he forced himself back toward the smell
of tarts at the bakery. He was sure that he could not
trust any of the teachers at school to help him with
what he planned, and so he politely asked the bakery
woman if she would write a letter for him from his
own words.

"Papa," he dictated in a trembling voice, "please

come and take me home at once. The school is cold, and there are not many books to read. Only three. People do not seem to like me here. Your loving son, Louis."

Yet once the letter had been written and the bakery woman offered to post it for him, Louis could only fold it into his pocket and give her his thanks, instead.

"You are not positive that you want your papa to come?" the woman asked him.

"At home, where I live, there are no books for blind boys," Louis answered. "I would never learn to play the piano or to speak in Latin words. I want to go home—I do!—and still I want to stay."

The woman pressed a warm almond cookie into his hand. "It is hard enough for an ordinary boy to be away from Mama and Papa, no? But the school *is* like a miracle to me, child. For years I have watched the pupils marching by or coming into my shop. So bright they are, like little tradesmen! The slippers and knitted caps they make are sold all through Paris. And I once knew the man who nearly starved himself to begin this school that you attend."

"You know him?" Louis asked. "You know Valentin Haüy? I've been told that the instructors at school will never speak of him."

"Jealous, that's what they are. They want to take credit for everything good at the school. But Monsieur Haüy had his troubles long before now, for no one wanted to lend him any money to begin his teaching. How that man struggled! And, mind you, he never gave up until he had a school for the blind. Then he was sent away by Napoleon after the Revolution. I hear he is in Russia these days, helping the blind boys over there."

"Why doesn't he ever come back to visit the school?" Louis asked.

"He's old now, child. The teachers don't want him back, and he knows it."

"But he must be a very great man," Louis said.

"*Oui!*" The woman nodded. "He used to bring some of the pupils into my shop, and he'd empty out his pockets just to buy them treats. There was a time when he saw blind beggars being beaten in front of the patrons of a café. Each beggar wore cardboard spectacles, Monsieur Haüy said, and a dunce's cap fitted with the ears of an ass. I doubt that the sight of those poor beggars ever left his mind."

Louis was thinking of Father Palluy. The Abbé and Valentin Haüy would have been the best of friends, he decided, if ever they had met. It was because of them both that he had come to Paris, and he felt suddenly ashamed of complaining about the things that had happened to him at school.

Wasn't he especially blessed to be given this chance to learn? Hadn't he always wished to do something useful and good? And now, with his prayers answered, here he was—pleading to go home like the little "baby Braille" that some of the older students called him. What if he did have to sleep in a cold, hard bed with porridge for supper that tasted like paste, and what if people did act mean sometimes? What about the *books*—the books, the books —the three heavy books with the big letters that were up in a room somewhere, just waiting to be read?

"I should be hurrying back to school," he said to the store woman. "They don't know I've gone."

She tugged on his sleeve and gave him a white paper bag. "Take these two more éclairs," she said. "I saw what those bullies did yesterday, and I told them that if they ever come back, I shall sweep them off the street with my broom!"

Smiling, Louis opened the door of the shop and heard the tiny chimes tinkling over his head. Outside, on the street, he clutched the pastry bag against the front of his jacket as he tapped his cane over cracks in the uneven pavement. At the corner, a passerby offered to help him walk to the other side, and he felt a gloved hand cover the top of his head like a cap and steer him gently past wheelbarrows and a horse that neighed in welcome.

He would be punished, he knew, for arriving late to Latin class, but he promised himself that he would practice all the verbs and nouns that had been given in the weekly lesson. And tomorrow, he would surprise the teacher by not making a single mistake.

❧ 8 ❧

THE BOY ON THE STEPS

The last lumps of snow had melted into dark puddles on the streets of Paris. Fountains began to spray their mist of water into the air, and flower stalls opened on the busiest corners. The cluttered old shops sold everything from parrots to printing presses to cast iron pots and pans, and barrels of pine nuts were set out in front of the greengrocer stores.

On the river Seine, unfrozen at last, bridges stretched like gray ribbons from bank to bank, and the sound of a new kind of boat could be heard that ran on steam and needed no wind to push it.

Louis had been at the Institute for nearly three months. Aside from his regular classes, he was tested with blocks of alphabet letters and, from the start, had been able to form the letters into words. Lessons began in ear training on the piano and the fife, and at a board of pear-tree wood he traced the engraved outlines of notes, key marks, and musical rests.

He was assigned simple work in the slipper shop, cutting the leather, and Gabriel taught him how to make a neck scarf with knitting needles and thick woolen yarn. Already he had impressed his teachers with his nimble fingers and active mind, and even Monsieur Dufau had to admit that the country boy from Coupvray showed unusual ease in mastering his subjects.

On Tuesdays and Fridays, Louis had one free hour before the supper bell, and he was finally given permission to take walks about the neighborhood by himself. Although the sights of the city were lost to him, he was learning to know its flavor with all of his other senses. He heard the coach horses on the boulevard, the click-clacking of the printing presses, the rustle of fashionable ladies who glided past him in their taffeta frocks. He could smell the live poultry in the store windows, and his fingers touched the stiff brushes that were piled in a hand cart at the end of St. Victor Street.

Near the Institute was a small chapel, set back from the street and surrounded by an iron fence. Sometimes Louis would lightly bounce his cane along the paint-chipped iron rails, trying out the rhythm of a school song he had learned. He liked to push open the squeaky gate when no one was near and to smell the rich perfume of rosebushes inside.

He decided on one of his walks that he might not be intruding if he were to step very quietly into the chapel garden, where Gabriel and Jean said that the roses grew as tall as their waists. Unlatching the gate, he turned inward, using his cane to judge the width and length of the stone pathway. The velvety buds on the bushes were spreading into blossoms, and the stems of ivy plants curled and wound their tendrils over the edges of the stones. But as Louis went deeper into the garden, he knew with that keen sense of his that somone else was inside, too. "*Bonjour?*" he said.

"You have a cane," was the reply. "Are you another blindy busting in on my spot?"

Louis raised the tip of his cane off the walk. "What did you say?" he asked.

"This is my place now. The other boy was trampled by oxen on the Pont Neuf at the river. He won't be back, and the chapel steps are mine. Go find your own."

Louis wondered if the voice he heard—and it was surely a boy's voice, not a man's—was talking in city riddles that he couldn't piece together. "But I'm just walking from school," Louis said slowly. "I don't think I know you."

"Bah—you don't fool me!" the voice answered. "I've tried all those tricks myself. Listen, I'm the only blindy working these steps—and that's that. Get out, or you'll be needing crutches as well as a cane!"

"*You* are blind, too?" Louis asked. His curiosity was overwhelming, and he put his cane back down onto the stones, ignoring the boy's open threat. "What work are you talking about? I don't understand. I'm a student at the Institute on Rue St. Victor, and, really, I was only taking a walk."

A long silence made Louis uneasy, but finally the other boy spoke again. "So, a little schoolboy! Well, I'm not in your fancy shoes, not me. I haven't got rich folks to put me away in there. I dump myself in places where people can see me, and I keep a cup ready for their coins."

Louis moved closer to the steps. "How old are you?" he said. "What's your name? Where do you live?"

"Are those the sort of questions they ask in school?" the boy growled. "I'm Josef, and I'm not sure just how old I am. Fifteen, maybe. Who knows? I live around the corner in a cellar—by myself."

"But where are your parents?" Louis asked.

"Parents! Parents are for infants—not for me. One night they took my brother and disappeared. They thought I was dumb, just because I'm blind. Ha! The very next day I found the broken window in the cellar and moved in. I made a bed out of old alley rags—and if the rats try and bite me, I give them a *whack* with one of my sticks. I don't need *anyone* now."

Louis's fingers brushed across the thick, fragrant

bushes until he felt the sudden prick of a thorn. Dropping his hand to his side, he barely noticed the throbbing. He had learned from his history classes that hundreds of men, blinded by the war, had settled into a life of begging on the boulevards of Paris. But somehow he'd always imagined that children near his own age would have someone to take care of them, just as he had his family back in Coupvray.

And yet, here was this boy named Josef whose parents had gone away and left him as if he were nothing more than a stray cat. *Blindy,* the other boy had said. The word sounded grim and terrible to Louis, and he shuddered against the warmth of the spring afternoon.

Maybe there should be an island off in the ocean, he thought, where all the blind people in the world could go and live. No one would make fun of anyone else, and Valentin Haüy could even stay there. He'd build a big school with his name on it, so that all the blind children might learn how to read and to become whatever they wanted—doctors or teachers or inventors of wonderful machines or harness makers or even learned priests like the Abbé Palluy. But not beggars. Never beggars.

"Josef," he said, "perhaps you could come and visit me at the Institute. It's not so awful there."

"You'll never get me inside that place," Josef said. "I hear that they throw you in a room and keep you locked up, with only dry bread for supper. If *I'm* hungry, I can find a better meal than that in the garbage piles!"

"But it's only the boys who misbehave that are given dry bread," Louis answered.

"No one will ever be telling me how to behave. I decide for myself."

"Well, perhaps you'll change your mind someday about the visit. And I shall bring some of my friends here to meet you."

"You know where to find me," the other boy said. But then he laughed bitterly at Louis's offer of friendship, as if there were too much pain in accepting such a rare and delicate gift. "Be sure to bring only your *richest* friends," he said. "They can keep themselves busy by filling up my cup."

Louis nodded and reached into the pocket of his trousers, although he felt afraid of what Josef might think. "I have one franc that you may take right now," he said.

But the beggar boy turned over his cup on the steps and scraped it away with his foot. "No! Forget it!" he muttered. "I don't want anything from you!"

Louis did bring Gabriel and Jean to meet the strange boy who practically made his home on the chapel steps. And he even spoke to Dr. Guillié about presenting a scholarship to Josef. But the director dismissed the idea at once. "What nonsense!" Dr. Guillié said. "We have enough students who can't pay for their studies. The Institute is not a haven for beggars. I have seen the boy you mention, and he is a ragged and surly creature. A scholarship is out of the question."

So Louis found that he could not really help Josef at all. He began to be plagued by the knowledge that blind people were suffering at that very moment in corners and alleys and cellars that were full of rats and disease—maybe even of death. On Tuesdays and Fridays, he was always drawn back to the chapel garden, if only to make certain that the boy was still there, and often he took the cookies that the bakery woman pushed into his hand and left them for Josef while his own stomach was churning with hunger.

When, in late June, he was given his chance to try the embossed-letter reading, Louis waited to feel the joy that he had expected would come at last. But as he turned the heavy pages of the one French grammar book or of the *Morning and Evening Prayer*, he would remember the sound of Josef's cup as it scraped across the chapel steps, and he wondered what would become of the beggar boy, or of Gabriel or Jean or himself.

The school term ended in midsummer, and Louis's few belongings were packed for vacation. At final ceremonies in the auditorium, he was awarded a certificate of merit in both knitting and slipper-making, and these were also packed in the old, battered suitcase that his father had made from leather in the harness shop.

Amid sad farewells to his friends, Louis brought the bakery woman an apron that his mother had sewn and sent at his eager request. Then he went to tell Josef that the school term was over. "I'll be back in October," Louis said. "And I hope you have a nice summer."

"I just may not be here when you come around again. I've heard about a better spot where another blindy used to work. It's near a school for deaf-mutes, and all the fancy ladies drop by to do their good deeds for the year. So, good-bye."

Louis didn't answer. But as he turned to leave, Josef said brusquely, "Take care of yourself. You're not able to scratch about the way I am."

The next morning, Simon René came to take his son home. And as Louis leaned against the warm, sticky seat in the stagecoach, he held onto his father's arm and felt more comfort than he'd known in many long months. Coupvray! Coupvray! the wheels seemed to screech as they rolled over and over on the gravel-studded road. Louis had marked off the coach stops in his mind—Nogent, then Chelles, then Lagny—and he knew that soon they would be home.

A hot breeze blew across his face from the open

window, and there was a lingering scent of acacia that bloomed in yellow clusters over the fields. "It smells like the country, Papa!" he said happily to his father. "Already it's as if I've never been away."

"But my customers, Louis, how they have missed you," Simon René told him. "They ask me again and again, 'Where is that boy of yours, the one who is nearly eleven and who beats you at weaving a fringe!'"

In the village square, family and friends, even the Abbé Palluy, came out to greet the stagecoach. The clamor of familiar voices made Louis suddenly homesick, and he had to remind himself that, indeed, he *was* home at last!

"You look so thin, Louis!" his mother said, half laughing and half weeping. "What do they feed you? All summer I shall have to fatten you up like one of the geese!"

"Tell her, Louis, that the school gives you food for *thinking!*" Father Palluy said with a chuckle. "I have heard that you did excellent work in your studies. So now, my boy, what can you say to us about this first year?"

Louis shook his head in confusion. What *could* he say? How could he explain? It was as if everything he knew about school was all mixing together in some kind of big kettle, as big as the one his mother used at home.

Inside were the cold and the dampness and the

loneliness of the dormitory when everyone was asleep. Inside were the few boys who stole and the teachers who rapped your knuckles and his disappointment over the slow, clumsy books. But, somehow, when he stirred everything up through his mind, in that make-believe kettle, the taste of school was sweet and good in his mouth.

"We're all of us the same at the Institute, Father," he answered. "That makes it easier to do things and to learn." Then, as the remembered sound of a beggar's cup scraped across his thoughts, he said, "I wish that every blind person could be as fortunate as I."

His sister Catherine gaily took his arm. "We're the fortunate ones, Louis. We have you home for more than two months! And there's news that might even rival the fashions of Paris! Did you know that Marie has a beau—and that his name is Françoise Marniesse!"

"Catherine!" Marie cried. "The whole town will hear if you talk so loud!"

And then young Simon added, "The whole town doesn't need to hear, *ma petite* Marie. All they need to do is see the way you blush!"

As the days of the summer sped by, Louis grew tanned and healthy in the clean country air. Perched on the steps outside the harness shop, he worked on the fringes again, and sometimes his brother Simon took him to nearby Chessy to walk through the vineyards that were for sale. There were visits with Father Palluy, and the week that he was taught to push the plow. Yet he was often restless that summer and would feel a swift, sudden urge to go walking just by himself.

As much as he loved being home, a part of him was uncomfortable with letting so many hours and days slip away. He found himself eager for October to come, for the touch of the few books that he could read, for the beginning of his second term at school. He told himself that there was something he should be doing, some work that was waiting just for him. But what was it, he'd ask himself then. What could it be?

℘ 9 ℘

THE VOW

A faraway clock sounded against the stillness of the darkened reading room. One—two—three—four muffled gongs. Louis's cotton nightshirt hung just below his knees, its frayed edges catching on the wooden shelf of the bookcase.

But the books on that shelf belonged to the sighted world, not to the world of the blind. They were printed for eyes that could see and were used by the staff of instructors at the Institute. Louis had such a book of his own at home—his book of lute songs—with thin, smooth pages and a soft leather cover.

At the table that ran the length of the wall, he opened one of the huge embossed-letter books. His fingers moved slowly over the raised shapes on the

page, circling up, down, and around the letters
H-I-S-T-O-I-R-E.

"*History,*" he finally whispered to himself. He
began on the next word, trying to identify the letters
more quickly. Today of all days, he wanted to read
without having to pause so long between the words.
Today was the twenty-first of August, 1821—and in
the afternoon a celebration would be given to honor
Valentin Haüy.

At long last, after fifteen years, the school was to
be opened to the aging teacher. A brand-new headmaster had replaced Dr. Guillié and had planned
a gala homecoming ceremony for Valentin Haüy.
For several months the students had been rehearsing songs and poems. Louis was assigned a part on
the fife and had been chosen with two other boys to
read from the embossed-letter books.

All week, in his excitement, he had hardly slept.
His father and brother were coming from Coupvray,
and after being invited for what seemed like a hundred times, even Josef had agreed to take one of the
tickets to the celebration. "But don't count on me
dropping by," Josef had said. "I told you I'd never
set foot in that school!"

"You don't have to go inside the building," Louis
had assured him. "The program is to be given on a
big platform in the courtyard!"

And the day was here at last, Louis thought, or
at least it *would* be day in just a few more hours.

That was why, even though he was supposed to be in bed, he had come tiptoeing down the hall to practice his reading.

Just thinking of the reading sent a queasy feeling into his stomach. What would he do this afternoon if the R's felt like K's or an A like an H? He might make so many mistakes that the new headmaster, Dr. Pignier, would have to announce, "I'm sorry, everyone, but Louis Braille is delaying our schedule with his clumsiness. We will not be able to listen to him read *one more word* from the book!"

Louis pressed his hands down on the heavy page. But Dr. Pignier would never say such a thing. He was always so patient and kind. He had forbidden the dry-bread punishments at school, and he encouraged the boys not to be afraid.

Still, to read in front of Valentin Haüy—the man who was known throughout Europe as the "Father of the Blind!" If only the letters did not have to be so tall and twisted! If only there were a way for fingers to glide across a page!

Louis carefully closed the book. Wherever he went, he seemed always to be thinking of how to read *faster*. He felt strongly that the blind must learn from their own books, ones that they themselves could read.

There were now eleven embossed-letter books at the Institute. The eight volumes that had been added since Louis first came to Paris were printed on an old printing press that was housed within the building. The students had been taught how to set the huge type and how to pull the wet sheets of paper off the machine. The raised letters could be printed on only one side of each page, and then the sheets were glued back-to-back in the proper order.

But eleven books against the millions of blind in the world? Eleven books with their bumpy, confusing letters, when boys like Josef had been left to starve because no one believed that they could reason or learn or be of some use?

Louis tiptoed back across the floor, staying to the side, away from the loose board that creaked. If I could just *do* something, he thought. If there were only some way that I could help. But perhaps Valentin Haüy would have new plans for the blind. And if Monsieur Haüy stayed in Paris, perhaps he could persuade the government to issue more funds for book printing and binding.

In the hallway, Louis heard the caretaker pushing a mop along the wooden stripping. "*Bonjour,* Monsieur Demeziere," he whispered, hoping not to get into trouble.

"*Mon Dieu,* Louis, but you startled me!" the caretaker answered. "What brings you out before dawn?"

"I woke up early to practice my reading," Louis explained. "I mustn't make too many mistakes when Monsieur Haüy has arrived."

"And just why is the smartest boy in school worrying about mistakes?" the caretaker asked. "Before you know it, the day will be over and you'll be riding home in the stagecoach with your papa. Now back to the dormitory with you, or one of the teachers will be catching you here in the hall!"

Louis nodded. "I am going!" he said. "*Merci.* But if you would, please say a prayer for me today!"

Monsieur Demeziere looked down at the thin boy in the cotton nightshirt. The blond hair was straggly; the pale face was ringed with dark circles under the sightless eyes. But the caretaker sensed that this twelve-year-old blind child was just the proper welcome for a man such as Valentin Haüy.

The musical program had never sounded more beautiful than on that hot, cloudless afternoon. Teachers and family members were seated about the courtyard, and the frail white-haired guest of honor was helped into an armchair that waited like a throne at the edge of the platform.

Louis had taken part in the counterpoint of drums, flutes, and fifes. But although he had not missed a note, his whole being was tensed for the moment that finally was drawing near.

The books had been placed on a table, and pages had been selected at random by volunteers from the audience. Dr. Pignier came forward to call out the names of the three boys who would read with the touch of their fingers, and suddenly the courtyard was hushed. Only a few ladies' fans whirred in the stifling air as students stood at attention on the platform, their crisp blue uniforms shining in the dazzling rays of the sun.

Louis linked arms with Christophe and Michel. At the rap of a baton, he walked in time with his two classmates. They stepped past the place where the sounds of their shoes echoed against the piano, past the place where Valentin Haüy would be sitting at that very moment, past the corner of the table to the long, wobbly bench.

Trying not to fidget or to make any noise, Louis waited for Michel and Christophe to read first. But as he listened to the halting voices of his friends, he was more fearful than ever of stumbling over the words and of sounding like an awkward child.

What would his father think then—or his brother, or Josef if he'd come—or especially Valentin Haüy, who sat close enough to hear every mistake?

Then Christophe shifted backwards on the bench, and Louis knew that his own turn had come. Touching the open book before him, he found the first complete sentence on the top of the left-hand page. Shakily, he began to trace the raised outlines of the letters, waiting until a word was formed in his mind before he said it aloud.

Letter after letter, word after word—carefully, tediously—until, at last, he was struggling through the final page in his selection. His throat was parched from the heat, but he drove himself on, reaching for the letters with his fingers, pushing himself to make sense of the slow progression of each sentence.

Five minutes passed. He had read two paragraphs on French grammar without missing a word, yet those two paragraphs had taken up nine pages of raised letters in the heavy embossed books.

With relief and some despair, Louis lowered his hands to his lap. The loud burst of applause and cheers from the audience consoled him a bit, but still he wished that he had not taken so long on the pages and that he could read in that soft flow of words that his sister Catherine and the Abbé Palluy used with their sighted books.

"*Vite*, Louis!" Michel whispered. "We are introduced to Valentin Haüy now—and this afternoon it's not just rehearsal!"

"But the sun is about to sizzle us!" Christophe said. "I would almost agree to be shivering on the very coldest night at school!"

Louis hurried across the platform. The months of rehearsing in the courtyard had given him, and the other boys, a sense of "motor memory." This meant that they could react automatically to the memory of how their bodies had moved about in the past.

Steps no longer needed to be counted on the platform, and canes had been deposited for the day under the dormitory beds.

Guided into lines, the students filed toward the armchair that held the bent but smiling old man. One by one, the boys were greeted by Valentin Haüy while parents and friends watched proudly from the lawn.

Louis straightened out the jacket of his uniform. But he was suddenly so tired and so hot that as he came closer and closer to the armchair, his legs began buckling under him. "Louis Braille!" exclaimed one of the instructors. "Are you ill? Here, let me help you down from the platform."

"*Non, non!*" Louis protested. "I will be fine, Monsieur Landresse!"

"But you should be sitting in the shade. I'll take you to a chair that is beneath the trees."

"Please, I do not wish to sit down!" Louis said. "I am feeling quite myself again. And I must meet Monsieur Haüy! I must!"

The instructor glanced toward the armchair. "Well, there are only a few boys in front of you. If it means so much, I will allow you to remain in line. But then you will rest?"

"I will, Monsieur Landresse!" Louis said. Swallowing, he felt as if he had been barely saved from a catastrophe. Why, he had almost fainted, hadn't he? After waiting so long for this day, he might have been carried right off the platform without *ever* being able to meet Valentin Haüy!

Moments later, he heard a low, quavering voice. "Ah," remarked the voice, "one of the young men who read from the books!"

Louis bowed at once. "*Oui*, monsieur," he said in awe. "My name is Louis Braille."

"You demonstrated the reading so well, my child. I can tell that you have studied the letters very thoroughly."

To Louis, the words of praise were like drops of the purest gold. "*Merci*, monsieur, *merci*," he said. Then he permitted himself to add, "But I know that if it were not for you, monsieur, I never would have learned to read at all."

"Reading is very important to you, is it?" Valentin Haüy asked kindly.

"It is what I like to do best!" Louis said. Then his caution seemed to entirely abandon him, and he blurted out, "Do you think that someday there might be books all over the world for the blind?"

"That was a wish of mine many years ago," Valentin Haüy answered. "But my books are too big for such a plan, and not every blind boy can read them as well as you. Tracing the letters takes so much time and patience. There must be a better way to talk to the fingers, and I pray that someday it will be discovered."

"But you may find it yourself, monsieur!" Louis said. "You have done more than anyone!"

"All in the past, my child. The days of work are over for me. I have lost the strength."

"Oh, but monsieur!" Louis began, and then closed his mouth against the rush of words. How could he plead with a tired old man who had already given so many years to the blind?

"Someone young and strong like yourself will have to carry on," Valentin Haüy was saying. "But this has been such a wonderful day for me. I thank you, Louis Braille, for your fine part in the program —and for your reading."

Louis felt his hand grasped between long, bony fingers. The touch was like the instant linking of a chain. Valentin Haüy's own hand was shaking, and the skin on his palm was wrinkled and dry, but Louis held on. And then, as the two hands unclasped, one old and one young, it seemed to Louis that the aged teacher had given him something to keep. It was a strange something that couldn't be touched with the fingers, but it flowed down into an empty place inside him and left him feeling full.

"I hope that you will be visiting us again," Louis said in a daze. Then he bowed and turned away, moving toward the steps at the platform's edge. A teacher was there to guide him down, and he heard his father calling, "We're over here, Louis! Wait—we are coming!"

He would take his father and Simon into the school building so that they might look at the decorations. And he must try to find Josef, so that his

friend would not be left alone in such a crowd. But, afterwards, there would be the swing and sway of the stagecoach ride, where time would stretch out like the long road home, and he could think about everything that Valentin Haüy had said. *"Au revoir,* Monsieur Haüy," he whispered back toward the platform.

"You were splendid!" Simon René said to his son. "Such music—and the reading most of all!"

"And to have been chosen from so many other boys!" young Simon told him. "What an honor!"

Louis leaned his head against the high seat of the stagecoach. "Next term, I shall learn to read faster," he said. "But I wish that Josef hadn't left without even saying hello."

Simon René shook his head. "I had no notion that the boy we saw was your friend. He was gone as soon as the program ended."

"I think he is afraid to come to school," Louis said. "But at least he heard the music. I hope he liked it."

"He owes you a great deal, Louis," Simon René answered. "Without you, he never would have found work in that bakery. He'd still be begging in the streets, wouldn't he?"

"Perhaps," Louis said. All at once the lurching of the stagecoach was making him incredibly sleepy. He half turned to lie down across his father's lap, just as he used to do when he was very small and was riding home in the market wagon at night. But he was older now, old enough to sit up like a man. He pushed away the lull of sleep and made room for the jumbled thoughts that had been reeling at him ever since the hot and exciting afternoon.

His hand still seemed to tingle from the grip of Valentin Haüy's bony fingers. But to think that Monsieur Haüy might be too old to teach and lead the blind any further! The students at the Institute had been told that their benefactor was working with blind boys in Russia. That work could have brought new discoveries, new schools, a new attitude from governments across the continent. But now—now there might be no one to wage the battle—no one at all. . . .

Louis touched his eyelids with the thumbs of both hands. *Books* were most truly the answer, he thought fiercely. *Books* with a new kind of reading for the blind. But who would find that new reading? Who— and *when?*

Then, against the stuffy warmth of the stagecoach, the words crashed at him like the beating of the village drum from home. "*You!*" the drumming said. "*You will find the way to make those books. You will be the one!*"

Oh, but I can't, Louis thought. *I can't. I am blind. How would I even dare to dream of such a thing?*

What of all the men, so much older and wiser, who have tried—and have failed?

Only moments later he jolted away from the dusty seat, nearly sliding onto a sack that was stuffed into the corner. But what—he breathed excitedly—if his blindness had taught him *more* about the darkness! What if he could understand the touch of fingertips simply *because* of the fact that his eyes were unable to see! Was it possible? Could this unthinkable thought suddenly seem so right, so natural, as if he had been waiting for it all along?

Yes! beat the drumming. *Yes!*

Dizzily, he began to know the meaning of the restlessness that always was lodged within him. There *was* work for him to do, a mission sent from God, a reason to want to read!

"Louis?" his father said. "Are you all right?"

"*Oui*, Papa. *Oui.*"

"Tomorrow, you can sleep until supper is on the table!" Simon René told him.

Yet Louis knew with a sudden certainty that he would not be sleeping past the rooster's early call. For starting tomorrow, he was going to begin his most important journey. And he would never be satisfied until he had made it possible for blind people everywhere to have their own books, and their own—libraries!—all over the world.

Yes, that was his vow to Valentin Haüy—and to

God. That was the work that would make his own life of some use.

There would be a new reading for the fingers, and there would be the miracle of many books—far, far too many books to put on just one table—and they would stand side by side on the shelves, and they would cast a great beam of light into the darkness of the eyes!

❧ 10 ❧

A ROAD TO FOLLOW

The cough simply wouldn't go away. Louis felt a
spasm rising again in his chest, and he hunched his
shoulders, braced for the hacking sound and the stab
of soreness that came whenever he climbed the
stairs or tried to run.

The dampness of the school building seemed to
have settled into his very bones. Even the thick,
fuzzy sweater that his mother had knitted didn't
help to make him feel warm.

He was convinced, however, that he had only
himself to blame for the cough. At night, he didn't
sleep well and would wake up to lie rigidly under
the covers, his eyes fixed in a sightless stare on the
patched, yellowed ceiling of the dormitory.

His mission for the blind had become an obsession

to him over the past two years. And now Valentin Haüy, the great and generous teacher, was dead. All that winter, Louis had felt alone with the burden of the darkness. He had not even allowed himself to confide in Gabriel about why he spent so much time by himself. He knew that Gabriel would only chide him for being "too serious" and for never really having any fun.

When no one was about, Louis would study over the geometric shapes that his father had cut out for him from leather scraps in the harness shop. Making rows of circles, squares, triangles, and rectangles on his bed blanket, he had hoped that these shapes might possibly be substituted for alphabet letters.

Letters, he had decided, were an invention for the eyes and not for the fingers. Most of the alphabet was too complicated to be easily understood to the touch. And because of their intricate lines and curves, letters had to be embossed for a blind person in oversized form.

What he must do, Louis told himself over and over, was to find some other sort of shapes or symbols. They would have to be easier for the fingers to understand, and they would have to fit into a space no larger than the tip of the thumb.

The geometric designs appeared to be a fine substitute at first. What if the letter A became a circle, and the letter B were represented by a square? But then he discovered that there were not enough shapes to go around. After circles, rectangles, triangles, and squares, he still needed over twenty different designs.

Climbing to the top of the staircase, Louis turned down the hall toward the reading room. His cough had slunk away for now, but he breathed in short and shallow gasps. Ever since morning, he had waited for a chance to reexamine the writing slate and stylus on the reading room table. He was almost glad over his bothersome cough, for Dr. Pignier had told him to stay indoors during recess period, and he would have the reading room all to himself.

Was it only yesterday that the writing slate and stylus were presented at assembly? Had only one night passed of thinking and planning about the papers that were punched with tiny holes and slits?

"The patterns of dashes and dots on these pages are a code," Dr. Pignier had explained. "They were made by fitting a piece of paper onto the slate and snapping a sliding bar across the top. Then a stylus tool was pushed through openings on the bar."

Louis had rubbed his fingers along the underside of a page, feeling the bump of the tiny marks. "The slate and the code were invented by a Captain Barbier of the Signal Corps," Dr. Pignier had said. "They cannot be of any real use to us here, but you boys may enjoy punching out little messages to each other."

Louis's hands had lingered over the slate before

he passed it on to Jean d'Anjou. "What are they going to come up with next?" Jean had sighed in disgust. "Letters out of pins, letters out of upholstery nails, letters out of wooden blocks! What's the good of it all? Even the books upstairs are only like big, silly toys for the blind!"

"But a code, Jean! That's something different!" Louis had exclaimed. "We can write it by ourselves!"

The students were informed that Captain Barbier had invented his code during the war. In the dark, when enemy soldiers might have been alerted by just the flicker of a candle, the captain was able to send combat orders that could be read with the fingers. He called his system "night-writing," with the more scientific name of *sonography*. And he had brought his code to Dr. Pignier, hoping to find fame among the educators of France.

Unfortunately, night-writing was far from an accurate substitute for words. The patterns of dashes and dots were made to represent *sounds*, rather than letters, and so proper spelling and punctuation were impossible.

"You will notice," Dr. Pignier had said, "that the code units take up so much space that fingering would be difficult in anything but the simplest message. But Captain Barbier has agreed to leave some of his slates and papers at school. I shall put a few on the table in the reading room if any of you would like to learn more about them."

Like to? After the evening meal, Louis had pulled himself up the staircase three steps at a time. In the reading room, he'd puzzled over the master code sheets and had punched dashes and dots onto paper. And all that night, he'd hoped with a desperately forlorn hope that Dr. Pignier might be mistaken about the uses for the night-writing code.

Today, he had come again to explore the pages with their punctured marks. Brushing his hands over a stack of pamphlets on the table, he began coughing hoarsely. But he kept sliding his hand along the table surface until he met the blunt edge of a wooden frame. The writing slate! He picked it up and hugged it to his chest.

Suddenly, an object rolled off the board. It flicked quickly across his wrist and fell to the floor with a sharp, staccato sound.

Louis stood motionless, frozen with a fear that came from not being able to see what he had done. Footsteps clicked down the hallway, and he heard Monsieur Dufau's voice ask accusingly, "Who is in here?"

"It is Louis Braille, monsieur."

The geography teacher scowled as he hurried into the room. "And why aren't you in the yard with the other boys?"

"I have a bit of a cough, monsieur," Louis answered, wishing that he could shrink into a spot on the floor too small for Monsieur Dufau to find. "Dr.

Pignier said that I should remain in the building today."

"So? Remaining inside means to keep busy with your lessons, doesn't it? Not to make a nuisance of yourself by sneaking around and dropping our equipment."

"But I didn't mean to drop anything," Louis said. "It was an accident, monsieur."

"An accident, an accident! Is that any excuse? You were helping yourself to that absurd writing slate of Captain Barbier's, weren't you? Now you've dropped the stylus, and you might have split it in two—not that that would be much of a loss, in my opinion."

Monsieur Dufau bent down to retrieve the pointed tool. "There *is* a small crack in the wooden handle! What do you think of that, you clumsy boy? If I had my ruler here, I'd rap your knuckles hard enough to make you more careful!"

Louis backed away, still holding the writing slate in his arms. "I'm terribly sorry," he said in dismay. "I only touched the stylus because Dr. Pignier gave his permision for us to examine Captain Barbier's work."

"Examine it, then! You will just be wasting time on another fool invention that's fit for the dust hole. Blind is *blind,* Louis, and you'd do well not to forget it."

The geography teacher flicked the stylus across

the table and then walked away. "If you need a hobby, Louis, you might busy yourself by making more hats and slippers or braiding the oxen whips that we put on sale. You owe us that much for the hours we spend on you. When no one is about to care for you anymore, all of your daydreams about book-reading won't put one thin franc in your pocket."

The door slammed, and Louis leaned dizzily against the table. Why, he wondered, did Monsieur Dufau dislike him so? Perhaps it had been wrong to make his vow, he thought numbly. Perhaps God was sending a message through Monsieur Dufau that there was more useful work to do.

A verse that Father Palluy had once read to him from the Bible came back in answer. He could still remember every word: *"Then God said, Let there be light; and the light began."*

Surely God must have wanted the light to shine for everyone, Louis thought as he groped for the stylus. And wouldn't He have meant for the blind to have their own touch of light? Perhaps Monsieur Dufau had never read that verse from the Bible.

Half an hour later, as the voices of his schoolmates echoed up through the corridors, Louis set down the writing equipment. The light would not come from a code of sounds, he realized with a final sadness. Dr. Pignier was not mistaken, after all. Yet the basic idea of the code—the dashes and dots—intrigued him. A group of them was small enough to fit under a single fingertip, and there might be some way to use them if he would just try.

He had entered the hallway when a flutter in his chest turned sharply into the tight clamp of soreness. Anxiously, he held his breath, but the coughing broke through, and he remembered how embarrassed he'd been in history class when his cough had made him flee into the hall to wait on the bench.

The coughing seemed worse now than it had on that other day, and he covered his mouth with his hands in order to muffle the sounds. His face felt hot and prickly, and he stopped to rest against the clammy wall.

Soon someone was climbing the steps toward him, and Dr. Pignier's voice said, "No better this afternoon, Louis? In that case, I believe that you should be in bed. I'll inform your teachers, and we'll see if a cup of hot broth will take care of that cough."

"*Oui,* Docteur," Louis gasped. "Please tell my teachers that I shall certainly be well by tomorrow. But the stylus in the reading room—I let it fall, and there is a crack in the handle."

"Don't worry over that, my boy. We have plenty of others. And knowing you as I do, I could have predicted that already you would be experimenting with the slate!"

Louis lay quietly in the dormitory bed for most of that afternoon, thinking of marks that could be felt with the fingers. Dr. Pignier wrapped a blanket around the iron headboard to keep out the drafts, and later brought up a chunk of fresh garlic and a tray with two cups of soup.

By the time the other boys had come into the dormitory after supper, Louis had found a slip of discarded paper on the floor and was using the metal prongs of a fork to punch patterns of holes.

When the night bell rang, it took every ounce of his willpower to put the paper away. Boldly now, the idea of dots—easier to make than dashes—was flashing through his mind like the flame from a comet in the sky. But he tugged up the covers around his neck, and weakened from coughing, he finally drifted off into a damp and fitful sleep.

Yet even in slumber, while others lay more peacefully about him, the vow was spurring him on. Over the bed sheet, his fingers tapped out a rhythm and promise all their own, punching and punching the imprint of tiny dots.

11

LOUIS AND HIS PINPRICKS

Monique unpacked Louis's suitcase, laying aside the garments that needed stitching or new buttons. She kept up a busy stream of conversation, glancing worriedly at the lines of strain and weariness on her son's face.

"You've won so many prizes, Louis!" she told him. "Geography, history, mathematics, piano. And to have been appointed foreman of the slipper shop, too! You must work yourself much too hard, *non?* Still, you have grown very tall this term. Why, you're a full head taller than I am!"

"I can't imagine how I grew even one inch"— Louis smiled from the stool—"without your cabbage soup, Mama, or your home-baked bread."

His mother reached out to stroke his pale, sunken

cheek. "If only I could say what it means to have you home again," she murmured. "And you certainly need a long rest. You seem to have a cough. . . . But what is this in your suitcase—a board and a tool that resembles one of your father's awls? What can you be doing with something so sharp?"

Louis jumped up, nearly knocking over the stool. "That's a writing slate and a stylus, Mama. Dr. Pignier let me take them home for the summer. I can handle such a tool much better now than when I was small."

Monique looked at his eager, outstretched hands. What she saw at that instant, however, was not her fifteen-year-old son—but a curly-headed child of three who beheld the world with wide blue eyes that were so soon to be damaged beyond repair. Feeling a familiar tug of anguish, she surrendered the slate and stylus to the waiting hands. "But what is the slate for?" she asked.

He wanted to give a plain sort of answer, one that wouldn't make his mother try and humor him as some of the boys did at school. Sometimes, when he requested more paper to put on the slate, a class-mate would poke him in the ribs and chortle, "Is it true that you really pour salt on these pages, Louis, and eat them just as the clock strikes twelve? Surely the food here can't be all that bad!"

And once when Monsieur Demeziere found the slate and stylus under the dormitory mattress, Louis had to persuade the caretaker that the equipment was not stolen, but had only been borrowed with the permission of Dr. Pignier.

"I'm working on a code, Mama," Louis said. "It might help us at school."

The family members gathered at the cottage that evening to celebrate Louis's summer at home. The table was piled with platters of fruit, deep dishes of cheese, stewed chickens, and slices of dark, chewy bread. Crowded around the table were Simon René and Monique, their older son, their two daughters and sons-in-law, their grandchildren, and their youngest child, who had returned from Paris in a tense and obvious exhaustion.

"This writing board that you have home," Simon René said to Louis. "Your mother tells me that you were working on it at the hearth all afternoon. Don't you think that you should rest a bit now that school is dismissed? Or even take a walk with the Abbé in our good country air?"

"It's the first vacation," Monique gently scolded, "where you haven't gone straight to the barn to pet the mare. She always senses when you've come home, Louis. I could hear her whinny from across the yard."

"I shall bring her an apple just as soon as supper is finished," Louis said with chagrin. "I don't know how I could have forgotten."

Catherine put a spoonful of grape jelly on her brother's plate. "While you were away, Louis, there was talk in town about the death of that lovely blind pianist, Marie von Paradis. People say that she was a close friend of the man who founded your school."

Louis nodded. Mademoiselle von Paradis had been a legend at the Institute long before her death. As a young girl, she had learned to read words that were punched into cardboard with nailheads, and she played the piano with such skill that Mozart had composed a piano concerto for her. "*Oui*, Catherine," he said. "Mademoiselle von Paradis and Valentin Haüy were friends for many years. She could dance the minuet or play a game of bowling, and she acted on the stage. In England, she even played the piano to accompany the Prince of Wales. Her blindness never discouraged her from these things."

"And you, little brother, you can do a great deal, also," Catherine assured him. "Papa says that at school you are an expert in everything! You must show me this curious slate that you have brought home."

"I had hoped to show you a whole new alphabet, Catherine," he answered softly, "just as you once taught me the letters from straw. I said that I would find an answer by last winter—and then by the spring. But now summer has come, and I haven't anything to show at all. So, you see, Papa should not be boasting about me."

"But, Louis, tomorrow might bring you your answer! Who is to say that it won't?"

His shoulders were slumped with fatigue. "The

days keep passing," he said, "and the blind are still thought to be half-witted creatures who should be thrown into the streets. And, for some reason, I have been foolish enough to believe that I could change all that. . . ."

Suddenly, he bolted from the table, his napkin dropping to the floor in a crumpled heap. He lurched across the room to the stairs, seeking a place where he could be alone and where his family would not try to reach through the unmovable wall of darkness that separated him from them. He had not intended to reveal so much of the mission that drove him through the days and nights and that had led him to fall asleep in his classes when there seemed to be no strength left to hold up his head or to listen to the voices of others.

Catherine pushed back her own stool and started toward the stairs after him. "What did I say that upset him?" she asked in distress.

The thick candle on the cupboard sent its wavering glints over the stairway as Monique answered, "It's nothing that you did, Catherine. He's so tired, and I don't think he's well. He hasn't been himself since he came home today. It may be best to leave him alone for a while."

Leaning against the stone banister, Catherine peered up at the garret. Then, smoothing her skirts, she slowly walked back toward the table. "He's not a little boy anymore," she said flatly, as if to impress herself with this new awareness.

"*Non*—not anymore," Simon René answered. "We will have to be very gentle with him this summer. None of us knows what it is to fight his battles."

The rest of the meal was eaten mostly in silence, with only an occasional giggle or whisper from the small children. But as Monique cleared the table of dishes, Louis came stiffly back down the stairs to say, "May I have an apple now, Mama? I should like to go out to the barn."

His mother stood looking across the room to where the night pressed blackly against the low window, and it seemed to her that a tired child with a cough would be more wisely tucked in bed. But then her eyes took in the quick nod of her husband's head, and she chose a large apple from the platter on the table. From habit, she polished the ruby-red fruit with the hem of her apron and then moved toward the staircase to give it to her son

Villagers who passed by the harness shop that summer often stopped to fuss over the lanky, blondheaded boy who sat on the steps near his father's door. A wooden writing board stayed balanced on Louis's knees, and in his hand could be seen a small pointed tool.

"So busy you are, Louis!" a neighbor might call out. "I strolled along Touarte Street this morning, and you were making your pinpricks on that board of yours. And when I am here again this afternoon, what do I find? Still you are sitting and playing the very same game! Your dear mother will be up into the night, rubbing the cramps out of your legs!"

Distracted, Louis would lift his head and then ask politely after the neighbor's family or farmland. But as soon as the footsteps or wagon wheels started up again, he would turn back to the slate, moving the sliding bar over his piece of paper to keep the punch marks in a straight line, and pushing the stylus through the tiny slits in the bar. How could he have told the neighbor that the pinpricks were a desperately serious "game"?

The master code of Captain Barbier's had required far more space than Louis wanted to use. Nineteen or twenty dots were sometimes needed in the night-writing system to represent only a single syllable of sound.

Louis was working with much smaller units of dots. He had tested out hundreds of combinations, trying to discover a simpler code that could be substituted for alphabet letters instead of sounds. But, always, if he managed to devise patterns for the beginning letters of the alphabet, he would find himself caught in the trap of having to form larger and larger units to represent the remaining letters.

When he was not working on the slate, he was haunted by the passage of months, as if time were strung out like rare, costly beads upon a measured string. Yet the slate and the stylus were like a part of him now, an extension of all his frantic prayers

and dreams. He had learned to punch dots or dashes into paper with the precision of a machine, and the tips of his fingers were nearly as sensitive as an insect's antennae, being able to "read" his half-finished codes with only the briefest touch.

His parents, however, worried greatly about him, even while he was under their watchful care. At lunches and suppers, Monique filled his plate full of meats, bread, and vegetables, and she went herself to the henhouse each morning to bring several brown, speckled eggs for his breakfast. And, as usual, the nourishing food, the radiant sun, and the clean air in his lungs turned him from a pale, thin city boy to a more robust child of the country.

But although the harsh cough had nearly disappeared and his face had rounded, Louis was still preoccupied and strained. He was home among those who loved him, yet he was not truly home at all. He preferred to sit with his slate on the stone steps or by the washhouse at the brook, rather than to join his father in the vineyards or to work on the harnesses in the shop.

"Perhaps we should not send him back to Paris," Monique said sadly. "It has never been Louis's nature to sit about and brood."

"But I remember when I was his age," Simon René told her. "All I could think of was having my own shop and being able to outfit every horse within miles. It's the same for the boy—except that he's dreaming of codes for the blind, instead of leather saddles. But if it will ease you, I shall ask for Father Palluy's advice."

Monique smiled sheepishly. "I already did so, Simon, before we left church last Sunday. Father Palluy talked of the scholarly monks who were with him in the order of St. Benedict. He said that Louis has been blessed with some of their very spirit and devotion. And I was quite relieved, until October started drawing near."

"School may be just the place for Louis now," Simon René answered. "Sometimes Father Palluy understands the boy even better than we do."

"But so many hours are spent on that slate, Simon! Our son used to be happy just feeding the birds, yet now he weakens himself with all this work. And to what end? How can he make *reading* for eyes that only see blackness?"

"The boy has some special gift," Simon René said. "I have always known it—from the time he was very small."

The gift that Louis had was perhaps a blending of courage, intelligence, and faith. But whatever its exact ingredients, that gift was finally realized in the waning days of the summer, as the dust blew in from the fields and the grapes were turning crimson or milky white upon the vines.

Somewhere in the village, near the shop most likely, or on the road that curved toward the brook, a new idea had come to him. He held it in his mind like a feathery flower that might wilt too soon, and then he began to translate it into the tiny punctured dots.

Patiently, he steeled himself for another failure, for the despair of having to begin all over again. But this time, he seemed to be plowing through the barriers that had confounded him before. Over the next week, he became so engrossed in his work that he forgot to appear for meals. Begging his parents to forgive him, he focused every particle of his energy on the idea that was emerging on the slate.

He found, with mounting excitement, that the units of this new code would fit easily under a fingertip. Instead of having to trace the tall and cumbersome shapes in Valentin Haüy's books or on Captain Barbier's samples, he could move his fingers across a page in much the same fashion as the eyes move along a sentence!

He checked over his work, probing for errors, but the tiny code signs were intact. Had he discovered it at last—an alphabet that might *truly* speak to the blind?

In a moment of delirious joy, Louis punched his own name onto the paper with a pattern of dots. Then, pressing down on the stylus in rapid succession, he spelled out, in code, *Mother, Father, Simon, Catherine,* and *Marie.*

A sudden exhaustion swept over him, born of

three years of almost constant effort. Carefully, he put aside the slate to lie back against the coarse stone steps of the harness shop. The sun warmed his face and neck, and he felt as if he were being released from his body, to float loose and free into the air. "I can write!" he whispered, thrilling at the enormity of those words. "I can write pages and pages! And then I can read them back with my fingers, as quickly as *eyes* can read!"

There were certain changes that Louis was to make in his code. At an early stage, he used some dashes as well as dots, but these were later removed. In its final form, the code was based upon a tiny cell of six raised dots that was three lines deep and two lines wide:

$$1 \cdot \cdot 4$$
$$2 \cdot \cdot 5$$
$$3 \cdot \cdot 6$$

Even a child's fingertip could cover the entire cell! Louis worked with only the top two lines, dots 1, 2, 4, and 5, to make the ten beginning letters of the alphabet:

A	B	C	D	E	F

G	H	I	J

For the next ten letters, he simply took the above code signs, and added dot 3:

```
    K         L         M         N         O
   ● ·       ● ·       ● ●       ● ●       ● ·
   · :       ● :       · :       · ●       · ●
   ● ·       ● ·       ● ·       ● ·       ● ·

    P         Q         R         S         T
   ● ●       ● ●       ● ·       · ●       · ●
   ● ·       ● ●       ● ●       ● :       ● ·
   ● ·       ● ·       ● ·       ● ·       ● ·
```

The letter W appeared very infrequently in the French language, and Louis did not include a W in his original code. (Later, he was to use a backwards R sign ⠗ for the W.) The patterns for the remaining five alphabet letters were formed by adding dots 3 and 6 to the code signs for letters A through E:

```
    U         V         X         Y         Z
   ● ·       ● ·       ● ●       ● ●       ● ·
   · :       ● :       · :       · ●       · ●
   ● ●       ● ●       ● ●       ● ●       · ●
```

Thus, by substituting the proper code signs for the alphabet letters, Louis's name would have been written:

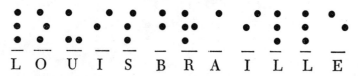

L   O   U   I   S   B   R   A   I   L   L   E

As he realized that he might adapt his dot system for musical notations, Louis thought of the book of lute songs that Father Palluy had given him. Someday, when he had the chance, he would make his own book of those songs. It would have pages punched with dots, and he'd give a copy to another blind boy to enjoy. Perhaps even Josef could learn to like a book!

And that wasn't all! Why, that was just the *beginning!* He would make signs for the numbers, and signs for the punctuation marks, and he would teach his code to his family so that he could write letters to them and so that they would know how to write in return! Yes, now Dr. Pignier wouldn't have to read aloud to him any news from Coupvray!

He shared his delight with his parents, heaping pages of code signs on the eating table. "Look!" he said. "This is the paper that you bought for me, Papa! I haven't wasted it! All of those little holes are writing that I can read! Anyone can read the pages, once they've learned my code! Do you know what, Mama? I can keep a record of everything that you need to buy at the market square! And, Papa, I can put up a sign at school, telling the boys about the best master harness maker in all of France!"

His parents laughed and cried, and he swung them about the room until he stumbled against the hearth and fell to the floor. But he waved off their concern and their helping hands. "I'm not hurt a bit!" he said. "Come—I want to show you how fast I can write my name!"

Louis could not have guessed that part of his name would eventually be used to identify the miraculous new system of reading and writing for the blind. So immensely difficult to create, *but so simple to learn,* the embossed code of dots would someday be known as *Braille.* The small unit of six dots that formed a basis for the code would be called the *Braille cell.*

And the genius of Louis's work would one day rank him with the greatest inventors of all time. His name would ring out with those of Einstein, Darwin, Galileo, Newton, Copernicus—men who also had given the light of knowledge to the world. But Louis was not yet a man at the moment of his great discovery. What was so astounding to many who knew him, and to many who were to learn of him, was the fact that he was only a fifteen-year-old boy.

Yet in that summer of 1824, the struggles of Louis Braille were far from over. He was to find himself with other hurdles to climb besides the invention of his code—for there would be people who did not wish him well in his fervent mission to liberate the blind.

SIX TINY DOTS!

"It works!" one boy whooped breathlessly. "I didn't believe it at first, but Gabriel Gauthier learned the code, and Louis punched out a whole page of writing, and then immediately Gabriel read it out loud!"

"Louis says that it will take just a few days to teach us his code!" another boy shouted. "And he says that we can keep our own diaries, and that if we all had slates, we could even take notes in class!"

The teachers at the Institute hurried out on the stair landings to try and stop the commotion. Hadn't the students been trained to be orderly and dignified young gentlemen? Feet certainly were not to run or skip in the corridors, nor voices to rise above a respectful or well-modulated tone.

Dr. Pignier had also opened the door of his office

to listen to the reckless and jubilant shouts. But the director made no move to discipline his students. In fact, as he saw their stiff-gaited skipping and their gesturing hands, his eyes glistened with sympathy and understanding.

Louis had already come into the director's office to stand hesitantly with the writing slate and stylus in his arms. "Docteur," Louis had said. "If you are not too busy, would you be so kind as to read me a short passage from one of your printed books? There is something that I have been waiting to show you."

Dr. Pignier agreed at once, and a volume of verse by the French poet, Charles d'Orleans, was brought down from the shelf. Leafing through the pages, the director had paused halfway through the book to read with slow and careful deliberation:

> *Time has lost her wintry gear*
> *Of wind, and cold, and rain,*
> *And is attired again*
> *In radiant sunlight, bright and clear.*

Punching and punching, Louis had been easily able to follow the pace of the words. After translating the final letters into code signs, he had slipped the thick paper from under the slitted bar on the slate. Then, with his sightless eyes seeming to stare up at a painting of ships on the wall, he had skimmed one finger along the underside of the paper. *"Time has lost her wintry gear,"* he began in a clear, unfaltering voice.

The book of verse had slipped from Dr. Pignier's hands to lie open on the desk. There, within the walls of the office, a blind boy was reading words as if his eyesight had suddenly returned to him! But how? What had this child done?

Dr. Pignier had asked to see the thick sheet of paper. Lightly, he traced his own fingertips over the rows of punctured dots, marveling at the tracks of a stylus that formed some ingenious new system of writing. "Louis—but this is wonderful!" the director said huskily. "Sit down. Please sit down. I want you to tell me *everything!*"

Eyes that can see, however, do not always have the vision of truth. Special slates were ordered so that the excited students could use Louis's code, and Dr. Pignier sent word of the discovery to the Ministry of the Interior in the French government. But when a group of society ladies came on tour through the Institute, holding perfumed handkerchiefs to their noses, they listened in puzzlement to the chatter over dots, dots, dots. "What are these poor creatures talking about?" one of the ladies asked Monsieur Dufau, who was leading the tour. "What are the *dots?*"

The geography teacher shrugged his shoulders. "Oh, nothing of interest, ladies. A trifling matter to keep the boys occupied."

Monsieur Dufau was not the only staff member at the Institute who tried to dismiss Louis's code.

The teachers could depend upon the familiar old books in the reading room, with their huge, embossed letters. But if dots were to replace those letters, the teachers themselves would have to learn the new language. And just suppose that one of them couldn't become accustomed to a new system and were to lose his job to someone younger with a certain aptitude for codes?

"That Louis Braille is a meddler!" Monsieur Dufau muttered in private to his fellow instructors. "He wasn't content with the books we gave him here. Let these blind beggars have a bite of food, and they ask for a banquet!"

Several teachers formally complained that Louis's dots were disturbing the classwork. The students, it was said, kept punching holes in paper instead of sitting at attention during lecture. But Dr. Pignier reminded his staff that sighted students usually took notes in class. "Louis Braille's dots can change every past method of educating the blind!" the director said vehemently.

Yet Dr. Pignier stood like a lone mountain against the tide of resistance to Louis's dots. While the teachers were fearful for their futures, the Ministry of the Interior stated that no changes in the school program were favored by the government. And then the business administrators of the Institute worried over losing their government allotment and having to rely on meager donations from patrons and friends.

Dr. Pignier was finally forced to tell Louis that the alphabet would not be given any official recognition. "But I'm taking it upon myself," the director added, "to let the students continue using your dots. And I shall write again next spring to the Ministry of the Interior."

"Perhaps, Docteur, if a blind person like myself could demonstrate the code," Louis said hopefully. "Perhaps if the Ministry of the Interior could just see how the alphabet works—"

"I understand what you are feeling," Dr. Pignier said, "for I feel it, too. You have worked so hard, and one has only to talk to your schoolmates to learn what the dots have done for them. But, unfortunately, the Institute will have to go on teaching the embossed-letter reading until we have permission otherwise from the government."

Louis did not want to seem ungrateful. At least the code could still belong to all of the boys at school. "*Oui,* Docteur," he said. "It is good of you to make such an effort in my behalf."

"But, Louis," the director answered. "I know what your dots will mean to the blind! I intend to help you in any way that I can."

Louis worked and reworked his alphabet, clinging to the hope that if he improved it, the Ministry of the Interior might find his samples worthy of notice. But months passed, then a whole year, and the dots were repeatedly ignored by French authorities. By then, Louis had transcribed two of Valentin Haüy's pamphlets into the code, a project that he saved for the night hours even though his old cough had come back and he was sometimes dizzy as he climbed the stairs.

Dr. Pignier tried to divert the exhausted boy's attention. Arrangements were made for Louis to walk each day to St. Anne's Church, where he received instruction on the organ. He was the first blind student to be accepted for study by the head organist, Monsieur Delacorte. And the fingers that could read dots with only the briefest touch learned to control the complicated keyboard with equal skill and grace.

At St. Anne's, Louis rediscovered the deep love for music that was rooted in the earliest years of his blindness. All of his longings found expression through the pulsing, melodic chords of the church organ. Bent over the keys, with his feet working the heavy pedals, Louis's entire being seemed to melt into the penetrating timbre of the instrument.

While the alphabet of dots remained in exile, "the blind boy from the Institute" was praised for his music by Felix Mendelssohn, the composer, and was offered an appointment as organist at a small nearby church. Although the pay was humble, Louis accepted the position thankfully—for it was proof that a blind person could hold a job of importance and be of use.

That proof was to grow when Louis reached his nineteenth birthday. With an opening at the Institute for an apprentice teacher, Dr. Pignier broke precedent by hiring one of his own blind students for the post. Even in the face of outraged objections, the director insisted that "conscientiousness, scholarship, and patience" had singled out Louis Braille for a career in teaching.

The news of the appointment reached Coupvray within the week. When a customer knocked on the door of the village harness shop, bringing a sackful of francs to pay for the saddle with gleaming buckles and dark, burnished leather, Simon René hurried outside to bestow the saddle as a gift. "Today I must repay God for His blessings!" Simon René exclaimed.

"You have had some good fortune, Simon?" the customer asked.

"The best that can come to a father," Simon René answered. "My son Louis has been made a teacher! Ah, and I knew it was to be, from the time the boy was a babe in his mother's arms. Even the blindness could not dull that spirit of his!"

Louis was issued a more elaborate uniform, trimmed with silk and gold braid. Although he was still subject to the rules of student conduct, he was allowed an extra privilege that he had never before experienced at school—a room of his own.

It was a small room at the end of a corridor, but to Louis, it was as immense as an arena. He rubbed his hands over the cold walls and corners, onto the iron bed and across the needlepoint chair. So much space! And even if he were a bit lonely for Gabriel, or if he missed the scuffle and bantering of the dormitory, he would be responsible for himself now —the true mark of a man.

He never folded back the bedspread during that first, solitary night in his room. Dawn filtered through a dusty window to find him writing in the chair, a sheaf of papers on his lap. He had spent so many other nights in an agony of fear that the government might never care to give further help to the blind. But, now, on this night—on the eve of his new responsibilities as a *teacher*—he had decided that almost anything was possible. Hadn't Father Palluy often said that progress could be as slow as a tortoise and that one must develop patience and faith?

Towards two in the morning, Louis had carefully begun work on what he had long been planning— a book that would explain his alphabet of dots. Somehow, he would find a way to have it published on the school printing press, and with Dr. Pignier's permission, he would keep it in the classrooms where he soon would be allowed to teach. Then, if the book were delivered to the offices of the Ministry of the Interior, wouldn't the officials finally have to give serious consideration to the six-dot cell?

Louis pushed back his doubts and fears, and tried to concentrate on having just a smattering of the Abbé Palluy's good patience and faith.

❧ 13 ☙

A PROFESSOR AT LAST

Two red-hot ovens filled the small bakery shop with the aroma of moist date bread. Louis took a deep breath, letting the warm air soothe the rawness in his chest. "It feels so good to be here," he said.

The old bakery woman patted his shoulder. "Josef and I thought you had almost forgotten us. But you are so busy, *non?* A brilliant teacher you have become, and a musician, too! The gossips report that you are invited to play piano and organ at some of the fanciest parties in Paris!"

Josef placed a tray of molasses cookies behind the counter. He had grown into a tall, broad-shouldered man who moved about with his head bent forward. "We keep a close check on you, my friend," Josef said. "We know, for example, that your students think you are the finest teacher at school and that every seat in your classes is filled."

"I have my sister Catherine's stories to give me help," Louis answered, "and so many Bible parables that I learned from the Abbé Palluy. Why don't you come and listen?"

"Now there you go again," Josef said. "After all these years, neither of us has really changed. You are the scholar—and I am still the street urchin."

The bakery woman brought in a loaf of the hot, spongy bread. "Don't listen to him, Louis. He likes to call himself a street urchin, but he can sort out the cookies faster than I can, and he bakes pies and cakes that are fit for a king. The doctor tells me to rest half the day, and Josef has been tending to the customers. He'll be managing the entire shop before long."

The date bread was cut into thick slices and coated with butter. Then the bakery woman shooed Josef out from behind the counter, and the three old friends sat down at a small wooden table to eat and to talk.

Louis was asked about his alphabet and his book with the long title. "What is it called again?" Josef scowled. "I can never remember."

Laughing, Louis said, "I can hardly remember it myself." Then he added with mock formality, "*Method of Writing Words, Music and Plain Songs by Means of Dots, for Use by the Blind and Arranged for Them.*"

"And this wonderful book of yours," said the bakery woman. "It has given you such pale cheeks, my child. Hasn't it at least unbent those men in the government even a little?"

"Not yet," Louis said quietly. "Every year Dr. Pignier sends a letter to the government. He requests that my dot system be made the official method of reading and writing at the Institute, but always the request is denied."

"Those government men must be blinder than you and I are!" Josef barked. "When I was growing up, there didn't seem to be any life but begging. You saved me from the streets, Louis, and now you are able to save almost *any* blindy from being ignorant. I'm honored just to know you!"

"And I, too," the bakery woman added. "Someday, Louis, the blind will be claiming you as their savior."

"But the alphabet may never be accepted," he told them both. "Captain Barbier was very angry when I sent him word of my debt to night-writing. He said that the dots were not as good as his own system."

"The captain is too eager to make a name for himself," insisted the bakery woman. "Don't pay him any heed. And, Louis, you must save yourself from so much worry. I will give you a big box of cookies to keep in your room."

On the way back to the Institute, a damp May wind swirled bits of paper and debris against the pants' legs of Louis's uniform. Drops of rain splattered down on his face, and a wagon clattered by with its driver muttering, "Sun one minute, rain the next. And I just put my *Gazettes* in the wagon for delivery!"

Louis tapped his cane more quickly along the pavement. Hunching his shoulders to keep the sharp wind from burrowing down into his collar, he felt a sudden wrench of sadness. He was twenty-two years old now, a man, and there was so much that he wanted to do. What had happened to his dream of libraries, with their great shelves of books for the blind? Was that only a child's dream, something that he must give up because he was no longer a child?

He was scheduled to teach grammar and arithmetic that afternoon, and he leaned into the wind and rain as if to push himself down the remaining blocks. Probably all the talk at the bakery about his alphabet had stirred up his disappointment over the years of refusals from the Ministry of the Interior and from the administrators of the school.

Yet there was another hurting as well that he couldn't identify. It tore at him all at once and burned more painfully than the knife of his constant cough. In mute alarm, he rushed past the narrow clutch of houses on St. Victor Street and up the steps of the four-story Institute building.

The downstairs hallway was chilled and silent. Then footsteps started toward him, and Dr. Pignier's voice called out in a strange tone, "Louis, may I speak to you for a moment?"

Rigidly, Louis waited by the staircase until the other man's hand touched his sleeve. "Your brother has come to see you," Dr. Pignier said. "It is unexpected, I know. He is in my office."

Simon? Here? "*Merci,* Docteur," Louis whispered, and then he staggered down the hallway, his cane scraping across the floor.

The doorknob of the office felt slippery under his fingers as he stepped into the room where he had come, trembling, on his very first day at the school. "Simon?" he said. "Is it you?"

There was a swift movement from the chair by the window, and Louis felt two arms wrapping him in an emotional embrace.

"At last you are back," Simon said with relief.

"But what is it?" Louis asked. "What has happened?"

The arms dropped away. "I wanted to be here with you, instead of sending word. Papa—is dead, Louis."

Out of the sudden numbness came a flutter of memories. Papa. . . . Papa in the leather apron, with the smell of brine on strong, thick hands. Papa letting him walk by himself to the market square so long ago, saying, "I won't be trimming your wings, boy. Not if you really think you can do it."

Gently, Louis was led toward the chair. "Your

name was the last word from his lips, my brother," Simon said. "He loved you dearly."

Louis heard another voice, dimmer than Simon's, a voice that was bursting with pride, telling everyone, "Louis is a teacher now! Geography, he teaches, and arithmetic, and grammar! A code he has invented for the blind to read! Soon he shall be a *professor* at that school!"

By late afternoon, the two brothers had made arrangements to leave for Coupvray. As the battered leather suitcase was hastily packed, Simon returned to the director's office to present a letter that had been dictated from the harness maker's deathbed. Across the page was an impassioned plea that Louis be kept in the care of the Institute and never abandoned.

"Tell your family not to fear," Dr. Pignier said to Simon. "Louis is adored by the students, and his record here has been flawless."

Conversation was meager in the stagecoach home to Coupvray. Withdrawn into his memories, Louis knew how fortunate he had been to have had such a loving and generous father. Another child without sight might well have been left to the charity of monks or to the cruelty of a band of beggars. How could his father be dead? Wouldn't the harness shop still echo with the deep, hearty voice or with the sounds of leather being cut into every shape and size?

On Touarte Street, the neighbors opened their doors to watch the arrival of the two sons of Simon René Braille. The older one, Simon, walked with an arm around his blind younger brother. Louis was moving with slow, dragging steps, his face chalky-white under the bright blue wool of his cap.

"What a grievous day for poor Louis," a neighbor confided to her husband. "I remember when he lost the sight in his eyes, and now his father is gone, too."

"But, then, he won't be left a pauper," the husband answered. "Simon René provided well for his family. Louis is to have the cottage, and most of the gain from the vineyards."

The body of Simon René lay on the bed in the cottage alcove. Lighted candles dripped their rivers of wax into flowered plates, and a curtain had been hung to cover the window. Louis kissed his mother and sisters, then went to kneel by the black-draped bed. Reaching out, he touched the arm that was folded over the chest—how still it was, how unmoving—and then, slowly, he lifted his father's stiffened hand.

"I shall miss you so, Papa," he murmured, rubbing the cold, roughened knuckles against his own cheek. "I wish that just for one minute, I could see your face."

A pressure on Louis's shoulder made him turn

from the form on the blanket. "Come," his mother said. "You must take off your coat. It is warm in the cottage."

He rose and drew his mother against his chest, stroking her fine, upswept hair. "Mama," he said, "we shall not let you be lonely here. All of us will help."

She cried softly into the folds of his coat. "You have given so much already, Louis," she said as she struggled to stop her tears. "All of your life, you brought your father and me such joy."

The spiced smell of the burning candles was hanging like a canopy over the alcove bed. "I don't know what meaning my life is to have," Louis answered. "But Papa once hoped that I would become a professor. Perhaps I can do at least that for him now."

Louis's appointment to a professorship came two years after his father's death. He received an increase in salary to twenty-five francs per month, and promoted with him were two other blind teachers at the Institute—Hippolyte Coltat and Gabriel Gauthier.

The three young men all used Louis's alphabet in their work, and there was a growing selection of classroom books that had been transcribed by Louis into the raised dots. With steadfast determination, he continued to provide reading material for his students and to increase his own speed at reading until he could decode more than 2,500 dots each minute.

The formal program of books at the school still rested upon Valentin Haüy's embossed letters, but in 1834 Dr. Pignier arranged for Louis to demonstrate his alphabet at the famous Paris Exposition of Industry. Visitors from all over the world came to view the exhibits, and many of them paused in curiosity before a blind, serious-faced young man who punched little holes into paper and then read them back with his fingers.

"How interesting!" people exclaimed. "How novel! Isn't he a clever one?" But even though King Louis Philippe of France had presided at the opening of the fair and had congratulated Louis on his invention, the dots were merely regarded as an entertaining game.

Louis's friends tried to console him. A party was held in Gabriel's room, and some of the young men who had left the school were invited to attend. Jean d'Anjou was there, and Michel and Christophe. "We are all your messengers, Louis," they told him. "We carry the banner of your dots with us, wherever we are, and sighted people will begin to notice. Soon, your alphabet will be used at other schools for the blind!"

But Louis was tired and weak. Ten years had passed since he had invented his code, and each year of obstacles and defeat had taken its toll. His lectures in the classroom left him short of breath, and students were often sent to fetch Monsieur Braille a glass of water for his cough.

Several months after the Paris Exposition, Louis went to bed with a fever. For two days and nights, he lay flushed and perspiring under the watchful eye of Dr. Pignier. Then on the third night, his cough was so heavy that he was forced to prop himself up against the pillow in order to draw a deep breath.

Shortly after midnight, an attack of dizziness seized him, and he felt his mouth fill up with a warm, foul-smelling liquid. Rolling off the bed, he crawled on his hands and knees toward the doorway of his room. "Can someone hear me?" he rasped. "God forgive me, but I think I am ill!"

The doctor who was called in attendance did not need long to diagnose his blind patient's sickness. All of the telltale signs were there. The fever, the cough, the exhaustion, the sickly pallor to the skin. And most of all, the dark red stains of blood spewed out upon the faded nightshirt.

"He has had a hemorrhage of the lungs," the doctor announced flatly. The illness was labeled "consumption," later to be known by medical science as tuberculosis.

Dr. Pignier had looked down at Louis's anguished face, passing a hand softly over the dampened forehead. "What should be done for him?" the director asked.

"We have no cure as yet. Fresh air, I'd say, and plenty of rest. I'll leave something for his cough."

Louis's teaching duties were reduced, and Dr. Pignier insisted that he take a walk each day in the air. Often, Gabriel and Hippolyte Coltat walked along with Louis, and the three professors would stroll through the botanical gardens or stop at the park to hear the ducks quacking in the pond.

Even in sickness, Louis never gave in to complaints or lost his own charitable nature. He began keeping his monthly earnings in an old wooden box, dipping into it frequently to buy small gifts for his friends or to purchase warm winter wraps for some of the poorer boys. Hippolyte Coltat was later to write in his memoirs that Louis "would have sacrificed everything for any one of us—his time, his health, his possessions."

When vacation arrived, Louis traveled home to Coupvray with his bottles of preparation for the cough. His mother devoted herself to nursing him back to health, laying out a blanket in the sunny courtyard for his nap and bringing him packets of herbs that she had purchased at a market stall in town.

He busied himself with transcribing, at last, the treasured book of lute songs from Father Palluy. With added symbols in his alphabet, he was now able to write musical notes in seven octaves and had made it possible for blind musicians to play the melody of a composition without ever having to commit it to memory.

When the book was fully transcribed, he sent one of the songs to Gabriel in a letter. "I trust that as Professor of the Music Department, you will sing this for me when we're back at school," Louis punched out in dots. "And if you ever come to visit me in Coupvray, I shall teach you how to milk a cow!"

Gabriel wrote back his thanks. "And if you ever come to visit me at my home in Paris," said the return letter, "I shall allow you to sleep in a quilted feather bed!"

But after signing his name, Gabriel had added, "I have heard a rumor here that Dr. Pignier may be in trouble at school. I pray that this is not true."

Stunned, Louis wondered what the trouble could be. Dr. Pignier had always been a respected and popular leader at the Institute. And he had befriended the dot system when other teachers and officials had refused either to look or to listen.

Louis hoped that it was not his dots that had made trouble for the director. He did not want to lose his dear friend. And besides, without Dr. Pignier's help, who would protect the alphabet from those who from the very beginning had wanted to see it destroyed?

14

DANGEROUS DAYS
FOR THE DOTS

Gloom had spread through the Institute, descending upon the chilly rooms like a fog. The old piano up at the stair landing sounded suddenly dull and off tune, and the trees outside were shedding their crinkled leaves until bare branches scratched at the windows.

Passersby on a certain Sunday might have observed the school director as he climbed into a waiting carriage, not turning his head to look back at the gray stone building where he had spent so many years.

Dr. Pignier's dismissal from the National Institute for Blind Youth was the result of a plot that had been formed in secret by Monsieur Dufau.

Sly charges had been made to the government that Dr. Pignier "corrupted minds with his history teaching." At that turbulent period in French history, when the nation sometimes functioned as a monarchy and sometimes as a democracy, the government officials were suspicious of nearly everyone. After a brief investigation, Dr. Pignier had been fired.

A new director was immediately appointed. By no coincidence, the honor went to the very man who had delivered the false charges—Monsieur P. Armand Dufau. Ambition and greed had steadily led Monsieur Dufau up the ladder of success at the Institute. First, geography teacher. Then, assistant to the director. And now the director's post itself. Monsieur Dufau would hereafter be known as *Docteur* Dufau.

Congratulating himself on his success, Dr. Dufau set about removing the one last obstacle that stood in his way. That obstacle was Louis Braille.

The Braille code of dots had already made the students more independent than Dr. Dufau preferred. Left unchecked, the new director told himself, it could have blind men taking over hundreds of teaching positions and musician's appointments in Paris. Although he was too clever to admit that he wanted the blind to remain helpless, Dr. Dufau took steps to insure his power at the school—and, once and for all, to put a stop to the alphabet of dots.

Louis was summoned to the office. In an icy voice,

Dr. Dufau said, "Still so pale I see, Louis. How is your cough?"

"I am feeling stronger, Docteur."

"Probably you would be healthier if you did not trot out so often in the night air to have dinner with Dr. Pignier. But I have called you here for more important business. There are to be a few changes in the school program."

A sense of danger prickled at Louis's spine. Ever since Dr. Dufau had become director, many of Louis's own students had been thrashed for breaking rules. The freedom that Dr. Pignier had brought to the Institute was now smothered by the punishments and harsh regulations of former years.

"Valentin Haüy's embossed letters will be modernized," Dr. Dufau continued with obvious relish. "I have just ordered a smaller style of type for our future books. However, it would be most inefficient to have three methods of reading at the school, do you not agree?"

"I— With your permission, Docteur," Louis answered, "I am not sure that I understand."

"Ah, well, that may be. To explain, I will tell you that I believe most firmly in neatness and efficiency, Louis. As soon as the new books are ready, the old ones will be destroyed."

Louis stumbled to his feet. "Destroyed?" he gasped. "But what do you mean, Docteur?"

"I am saying that, in the spirit of reform, I have

decided to burn all of the school's existing books."

Terrified, Louis felt an impulse to plunge through the wooden door of the office. His feet began to move as if he were already rushing up the staircase. He would twist past the curve at the landing, up, up, up to the reading room, where he would gather all the books into his arms until they were piled high above his head.

Then he would hide them! In a safe place, as his mother used to hide the money jar from the soldiers. Fumbling in his pocket for a handkerchief, he coughed deeply into the soft, yielding cloth. Oh, but he could not really do such a thing! The books were not his, not even the ones that he'd written himself, not even the new book that explained his dot method for beginners in arithmetic.

"And furthermore, Louis," Dr. Dufau said, "your dot code is no longer to be used in the classroom. The boys will turn in their slates and will concentrate on the embossed letters. It may be tiresome for them, but they will survive."

The words had struck at Louis like separate blows. Yet he knew that any pleas of mercy for his dots would only increase Dr. Dufau's pleasure. Nodding, he fled from the room and staggered out the front door of the building.

Pacing the streets near the school, Louis leaned heavily on his cane. *Please give me the strength,* he prayed silently, *to bear this one more burden.*

An hour later, he was wearily arranging his notes for a grammar class. "Monsieur Braille," said a sudden voice at his side, "my father will be able to send me the funds for my tuition. And I can repay the loan that you so kindly made me!"

"That is fine, Jacques," Louis answered. "We shall take your name off the slip of paper in my little wooden box."

"I hope to become a teacher just like you, Monsieur Braille!" the boy said. "I have been keeping a notebook of what I learn here at school, and I punch out the dots very quickly now."

Louis winced against the searing pain in his chest. "It might be wise, Jacques," he said softly, "to let your family guard such a valuable notebook at home."

The books that Louis had so diligently transcribed into the dots were burned in a blazing fire at the back of the courtyard. Along with them went slates, styli, and Valentin Haüy's embossed textbooks. And when nothing but ashy flakes and bits of metal were left to scatter across the ground, Dr. Dufau had ordered the caretaker to "sweep away this soot at once!"

But neither Louis nor Dr. Dufau had ever supposed that another fire was burning within the hearts of the students. Milling about in the halls and dormitory, the boys made whispered plans to fight for their cherished dots. The books, slates, and styli might have been destroyed—but Dr. Dufau was to learn that an *idea* could never be burned and that *knowledge* could not be put into bondage.

Within days, a mutiny had broken out at the school. In wonderment, Louis heard that the students were slipping pencils, nails, forks, and knitting needles into their pockets, searching for anything thin and sharp that would punch out the dots onto paper.

Angrily, Dr. Dufau kept issuing his demands, but none of them was followed. One of his assistants, a man named Gaudet who was sympathetic to the students' cause, said that cutting off the dots was like cutting the wings from a bird that had been yearning to fly. "The blind can truly read and write with the Braille alphabet," Gaudet told the director. "And that is a privilege, Docteur, which our students are not willing to give up."

Dr. Dufau sputtered and scowled and listed all the other systems for finger reading that had been invented since Louis first devised his six-dot cell. "We can't allow every blind child to learn a different method!" Dr. Dufau said defiantly. "Who knows which is best?"

"The *boys* have said which is best," Gaudet answered. "The other systems use a form of regular alphabet letters, mainly because inventors have been trained from childhood to think in terms of letters.

But Louis's dots solve the problem in a way that makes sense to the blind!"

Then Gaudet added, "The situation is quite beyond our control, Docteur. The students are not going to accept your ban on the dots. Rumors of the unrest are already reaching government ears."

If there was one problem that Dr. Dufau did not want, it was trouble from the government. Perhaps Louis Braille was not so easily disposed of, after all. "Enough! Enough!" he snapped. "I will lift the ban on the dots. Let the students have their foolish punching! There is other business on my desk that needs attention."

Gaudet turned to leave. "*Merci,* Docteur," he said with relief.

Dr. Dufau waved an envelope in front of his assistant's face. "By the way, Gaudet, we have received permission to plan for the construction of a new Institute building. That should make the little rebels happy!"

On November 11, 1843, a new building for the blind was completed at No. 56 Boulevard des Invalides. Through family and friends, the students had uncovered a few copies of Louis's dot books and planned to bring them into the larger reading room at the school.

The boys felt great pride in the clean, airy quarters of their new home. "Tell us how everything looks! Tell us!" they begged their sighted teachers, and then listened raptly to the description of the brick arches over the windows, the sturdy turret on the roof, the tall iron fence with its two lanterns, and last but not least, the waving majesty of the French flag that jutted out from the front of the building.

Emotions were mixed, however, on that November day when the old building was finally left to its dusty cobwebs and its dank, crumbling walls. The students had grown accustomed to the touches, smells, and sounds of their first school, just as a sighted person will come to know the look of a familiar place. Yet for the blind, what is familiar is most especially prized, and so there were tears and regret as well as excitement when the boys were led in a last procession from St. Victor Street.

At the new building, clothing was unpacked into drawers, and suitcases were stacked away in a storage closet. Then excitement reigned completely as the boys found a welcoming present from Gaudet on the end of each dormitory bed. The surprise gift was a rectangular object, made of wood. On the top was a slitted metal bar that moved up and down over a heavy piece of paper.

"New writing slates!" the boys shrieked. "We've beaten Dr. Dufau! We've won! We've won!"

Up in his room, Louis had received a present of his own. Two history books had been delivered from

Dr. Pignier, transcribed into dots by the former director. Enclosed was a note in the dot code, which said, "To Louis—who has helped us all to *see*."

In February, the Institute on the Boulevard des Invalides was officially dedicated. By this time, the students had signed a handwritten petition, which they sent off to the government. The paper asked that the French Legion of Honor be awarded to a blind professor named Louis Braille—in appreciation for his invention that had made knowledge and communication possible for the blind.

None of the officials seriously considered the finger-smudged petition. They thought it absurd and utterly preposterous, although they were reminded that samples of the code had been filed away in the backs of their cabinets. But when these same officials arrived for the dedication ceremonies, to be seated with teachers from all parts of France and with members of the Chamber of Deputies, they were told that the dot code—*Braille,* some people were calling it—was to be demonstrated through the efforts of the assistant director, Gaudet.

While Louis sat in the front row of the auditorium, his legs trembling so hard that his knees kept knocking on each other, one of the officials was summoned from the audience. The gentleman was given a verse of poetry to read aloud. Then a pretty little girl with blond pigtails and large, blank staring eyes stepped onto the stage.

Girls had been admitted as students for the first time in the Institute's history. The blind child listened to the poem with her pigtails swaying and her hand rapidly punching a stylus onto a papered slate. After the official had fully recited the verse, the child touched the dot marks with her fingertip and repeated the exact words in a lisping, singsong voice.

Applause from the audience reached such a crescendo of sound that several teachers clocked six minutes before the thunderous clapping had faded away. Many of the invited guests knew of other inventors' attempts to make reading and writing possible for the blind. They had seen children's fingers trying to follow the twisted outlines of alphabet letters or to unravel the confusing symbols for syllables of sound. But this girl on the stage had so easily recorded the poem and then had read it back as if she could actually see!

Suddenly, a balding official came into the center aisle. "We are certainly impressed," the official remarked. "But how can we be sure that this child did not memorize the poetry in advance?"

The man was resoundingly booed by the audience, but Dr. Dufau walked speedily across the stage. As if the dots were his personal invention, the director said, "Now, now—I would not wish to receive any credit for this performance until we are all convinced of the truth. Would the gentleman in the aisle care to read from some writing that he carries on his own person?"

The official dug into his pockets and found a ticket stub from the opera. Clearing his throat, he read off the name of the theater, the address, the date, the time, the seat number, and a statement of policy regarding cancellation of tickets. But even before the man had returned to his seat, he heard the little girl repeating the information from the stub.

This time, the audience jumped from their chairs to cheer, clap, and stomp their feet. "The inventor! Who is the inventor?" came the cries.

Before Dr. Dufau could say a word, Gaudet had announced, "The inventor is a professor from the Institute, a man who was previously one of our own students. His name, ladies and gentlemen, is *Louis Braille!*"

Louis was asked to stand, and the applause burst forth again. Friends and strangers hurried to shake his hand, to pat him on the back, to ask him nine or ten questions all at once. He did not leave the auditorium until just before dinner. By then, Gaudet had come to tell him news that left him weak. "Your alphabet will at last be accepted for the reading program," Gaudet said. "After the demonstration, the government officials have admitted that it is time for a change."

In the dusk of that February evening, Louis walked alone to the place where, even to the sighted,

messages from the heart were more important than those from the eyes. The small corner church had once employed him as an organist, but he had given up the position to a blind student who needed the money.

Soberly, he knelt in the pew and offered his ardent thanks to God. A victory had come, and he rejoiced in it more for all the blind children of the alleys than for himself. "I shall use whatever days are left to me," he whispered to the presence of the faith that was within him, "to continue with our work."

The peace and silence of the church infused him with a feeling of great love and gratitude. He did not rise from his knees until the bells rang out for evening vespers, and as he started back toward the Institute, his string of rosary beads was tightly gripped in his hand.

His fingers touched the beads, one by one. He was remembering all the people who had believed in him and whose belief had never seemed to waver. The Abbé Palluy, who had just recently passed away, leaving so much goodness behind in his acts of mercy, and Dr. Pignier, and his fine friends, such as Gabriel, Josef, and Hippolyte. His brother and sisters, his gentle mother, and the blessed memory of a father who was generous, true, and kind.

Louis's fingers, the fingers that had wrought a miracle, reached up to touch the beads against his lowered eyelids. It was his thirty-sixth year, and he had not seen the sky, the trees, or the grass since he had been a child of three on a spring day in a village harness shop.

But even though his eyes could not tell him of men or events, of doctrines or ideas, he had found another way—for himself and for others—to know the glory of such things.

❧ 15 ❧

LIGHT FOR THE BLIND

On the desk in the reading room was a machine with levers and round metal keys for punching. Louis had invented this strange apparatus with another blind man named Pierre Foucault, and with it a message might be sent that both blind *and* sighted persons could read!

The message appeared in alphabet letters that were shaped by raised dots instead of being printed in ink. Louis and Pierre Foucault had called their printing method *raphigraphy*, and their machine was much later to be hailed as a primitive version of the typewriter.

Louis punched the proper keys to begin his letter to his mother. "Dearest Mama," he wrote, but then he shook his head and leaned back against the rungs of the chair. Sometimes, when he tried to concentrate, the dizziness spun his thoughts into vague, fuzzy wads, like pieces of cotton stuffing.

Still, he consoled himself, the coughing had lessened in the last six months. Hadn't the doctor pronounced him well enough from the dreaded consumption to resume his teaching? And hadn't the board of administrators granted him a permanent home at the Institute? He would not have to leave his students after all, and he might remain quite near the reading room—even though it had not yet grown into a library full of many, many books for the blind as he had dreamed.

Outside, Louis heard the thudding roar of a cannon, followed by shouting on the streets. His expression grew grave as he felt a surge of kinship to his country. He, too, had known the wars of suffering and unrest.

Boots had tramped long ago on the cobblestones of Coupvray when he was just a child. And now, in 1848, France was split by another violent revolution. King Louis Philippe, who had once spoken kindly to Louis at the Paris Exposition of Industry, had been torn from his throne after a fifteen-year rule. Revolutionaries had overrun the palace, declaring a republic in the name of freedom.

Louis approved of the new, democratic ideals for France, but he was glad that the king had escaped injury by fleeing to England. Many of the teachers and students at school argued heatedly over politics. Gabriel had composed a triumphal march in honor of the new republic, and the hardier blind students had planted trees in the courtyard while singing of France as "queen of the world."

Louis turned back to his letter to his mother. "I was so pleased," he punched out on his machine, "to hear that the weather had kept fine for the vintage, or at least as fine as could be expected. But now the days are drawing in. Winter has begun and one should stay indoors. I do not go out, and while Parisians are celebrating the new Constitution in a snowstorm, I was glad to sit snug in my warm little room and listen to the cannon.

"Well, let's keep smiling and get through the winter. Write to me and tell me how my family and friends are getting on. I hope to come and see you once winter is over.

"Until that happy time, I remain your loving son, Louis."

The winter snows and his failing health kept Louis more and more in the safety of his room. Calling on strength that he did not have, he would come resolutely down the halls to teach his classes, and in the evening he might sip a cup of mint-flavored tea with Gabriel and Hippolyte. But mostly he devoted himself to transcribing complex musical scores into the dots or sending books to be copied by some of his former students.

Although the dot alphabet had barely penetrated beyond the walls of the Institute, Louis took solace in the signs that a new world was beginning to open for the blind. The Book of Psalms had been printed by means of six-dot type facings, and prayer books for chapel services had been issued in the code.

In the next two years, however, Louis was again so weakened by the ravages of his illness that he asked to be retired from teaching. His classes were assigned to another man, but his name was retained on the faculty roster, and an opportunity was left open for him to give piano lessons if he should regain his strength.

He traveled home to Coupvray whenever he was able, cheering his mother with assurances that her cabbage soup from the old kettle was still the best nourishment anywhere. Two of his nephews were carrying on the trade in the harness shop, and Louis often stood with nostalgia in the cool stone room, hearing the faint memory echoes of his father's mallets and awls. The thick hooks near the window were easily reached by his fingers, but he would recall the days of his youth when he had stretched up on tiptoe and still could not touch the marvelous hangings of straps, collars, and reins.

Just before Christmas of 1851, he went to walk among the brownstone shops in Paris that were fairly bulging with gifts for the season of giving. An aproned shopkeeper bustled forth to push into his hand a small painted statue of the baby Jesus. "Bless you," the shopkeeper had said, and Louis's sensitive fingers had traced over the tiny ceramic infant in its folds of swaddling clothes.

But on the evening of that walk, his cheeks had flamed from the outing in the cold, and he found that he could not lie down without a band of pain squeezing across his shoulders and back. Before the night was done, he was admitted to the school infirmary in a spasm of coughing.

His friends and dozens of his students came, frightened and sleepy, to cluster by the door of the sickroom. Gabriel, and then Hippolyte, were allowed a few moments by the bedside.

A nurse was lowering a tray of medicines onto a metal cart. "He is hemorrhaging badly," she whispered to the two friends, who could not see her patient's ashen face and red-stained sheets.

Louis raised himself with effort from the pillows. "Gabriel? Hippolyte?" he asked. Then he said calmly, "Please—both of you—do not fear for me. I am quite content. God simply must be telling me that my work here is finished."

"But you will be fine, Louis!" Gabriel said.

"You'll be walking with us in the gardens before long," Hippolyte exclaimed. "And there is still so much for you to do with your books!"

Louis smiled. "Others will carry on for me," he said, "just as I once tried to carry on for someone else. . . . Why, do you suppose that I shall be meeting Valentin Haüy now? Neither of us accomplished exactly what we'd hoped. But what a conversation we might have this time!"

By morning, Louis had asked to receive Holy Communion. He was breathing heavily as a priest was summoned from down the street. Dr. Pignier and Josef came to keep a sorrowful vigil at the bedside, and although Louis's mother was too ill herself to make the journey from Coupvray, Simon was expected in several hours.

For over a week, however, as the bells of Christmas rang out from all the great towers of Paris, Louis clung to life in the infirmary bed. The majestic pealing of the bells stirred his imagination back to the winter when the Abbé Palluy had come to the cottage on Touarte Street with news of a school for the blind. "The instructors at this school have learned a way of teaching the blind how to read!" Father Palluy had said, and Louis still thrilled to the sound of that splendrous word.

Read! Read! The word had pealed through the tiny cottage room, and once more it rang out in Louis's ears—softly to the bell sounds from a far-off tower, grandly to the bells of spires that pointed their golden tips above the river Seine, richly, with heartfelt reverence, to all the bells of churches big and small that graced the streets of the city.

On January 6, two days after Louis's forty-third

birthday, he again asked to receive Holy Communion from a priest. Simon held his brother's hand through those final hours, while the agony of the wracking cough was borne with no despair by the gaunt figure on the sheets, but only with charity toward those who stayed to comfort him and with faith for what lay ahead.

A notary was called to record Louis's last will and testament. He did not forget any of his relatives or friends, no matter how small the bequest. Even the night watchman, the servant who cleaned his room, and the orderly in the infirmary were to receive a remembrance. Then, as breathless messages of endearment for his mother and for his family were entrusted to a tearful Simon, the clock bells chimed out the half hour after seven. At that very moment, a gentle and victorious spirit withdrew from the room.

Hippolyte Coltat was to enter later in his own diary that "Louis Braille [had] delivered up his pure soul to the hands of God."

Funeral services were held at the National Institute for Blind Youth on January 8, 1852. Afterwards, Louis's body was taken on its final trip through the frost-layered countryside.

The deserted fields were asleep under the spell of winter. Once, however, they had brought the scent of wild strawberries and clover, of milfoil and acacia to a young blind boy in a stagecoach, while birds had chirped their greetings from the trees and fishermen had called up from the banks of the river Marne.

Simon kept a protective hand on the lid of the coffin, as if he were still watching out for the little brother who could not see. At the humble cemetery in Coupvray, Louis was buried while the saddened Braille family mourned his death. Yet, in Paris, newspapers did not carry even the smallest mention of the passing of the blind professor who had invented such a remarkable alphabet of touch.

As with so many other great geniuses and creators, Louis Braille had died without the recognition that he deserved. The world was yet to realize that when a fifteen-year-old harness maker's son had punched out his pinpricks, a new highway to the mind was forged through the darkness.

The dots would win fame for themselves and their inventor, but only after three more decades of resistance and struggle. In the aftermath of Louis's death, a few crusaders took the alphabet under their wings, and the Lord's Prayer was issued by means of the dots in English, Italian, Latin, Spanish, and German. But some of the countries made confusing changes in the six-dot code. The British used three different "grades" of Braille dots, while America introduced a system of her own called New York Point.

Loyalties were stubborn, and tempers were thin.

Only a small number of books was printed under each system, and the competition grew fiercer by the year. As a result, the task of educating the masses of the blind stayed dismally at a standstill.

At last came an important breakthrough. A school in St. Louis, Missouri, discovered that a blind student could read much faster by Braille than by New York Point. After testing every existing method of finger reading, the directors of the St. Louis school chose the Braille alphabet for their students.

Far away in Peking, China, a Scottish missionary was also working with the blind. W. H. Murray had studied more than 4,000 letter characters of the Chinese language, reducing them to just 408 sounds. He appointed a number to each sound and wrote down the numbers in Braille. Even a language as difficult as Chinese could be translated into Louis's dots!

Twenty-four years after the death of the gentle blind professor, an international Congress of Teachers of the Blind met in Dresden, Germany. After days of debate, the teachers voted to support one of the modified versions of Louis's code. But several educators warned that only the original alphabet, as invented by Louis Braille himself, would meet all the tests put to it.

Not surprisingly, in 1879 the congress changed their decision. They recommended that the original six-dot alphabet, the *Louis Braille alphabet,* be used in schools for the blind throughout the world.

Today, the magic dots are truly the universal language by which the blind can read and write. Sightless children from all parts of the globe—from Egypt, India, Israel, Canada, Scandanavia, Viet Nam—have their special story books whose pages appear to be sprinkled with the raised white dots.

In the village square of Coupvray, a monument now stands in honor of Louis Braille. Carved into its stone base are the words, *A Braille, les Aveugles Reconnaissants*—or, *To Braille, the Grateful Blind.*

The genius of the brilliant Frenchman finally had captured the attention of the world. On the hundredth anniversary of his death, the newspapers that had once ignored Louis Braille were splashed with headlines of his burial in a new resting-place. On June 20, 1952, Louis's body was removed from the simple grave at Coupvray and laid in a huge double coffin. Thousands of blind from near and far helped escort his body to Paris, and there the procession was joined by notables of forty different countries.

Walking behind the horse-drawn casket, the great crowd of people grew larger and larger as Parisians came from their houses to pay their respects to Louis Braille. The casket was lifted up the steps of the Pantheon building, to receive the highest honor that

France can bestow upon its dead—burial among the most famous heroes of the nation.

Yet Louis did much more than lead a heroic life. He earned the distinction of having changed the course of civilization by reaching into the minds of his blind brothers. His dots are now typed by special Braille machines or translated onto belts of tape by computers, and his books are stocked in many public school classrooms—for use by blind children who are no longer educated apart from their sighted friends.

At the growing number of volunteer organizations for the blind, a visually handicapped person will almost always receive any book that he requests— even if only a single copy is needed. Volunteers have transcribed everything from piano concertos to best-selling novels to a city telephone directory for a blinded salesman.

Some organizations distribute dotted Christmas cards, games, clocks and wrist watches for the blind. Schools, streets, and publications have been named for Louis Braille, and in 1948 a French postal stamp was issued that was decorated with his picture. His name, in fact, is so indelibly connected with the system of raised dots that *Braille* is usually listed in dictionaries without being capitalized.

Yet of all the honors paid to him, none would have pleased Louis as much as the worldwide libraries for the blind. How he would have loved those great shelves of books! It is almost possible to imagine his pale, eager face aglow with the fulfillment of his vow. Just as when he stood in the study of the old presbytery at Coupvray, Louis would surely fling out his arms to embrace the rows of glorious books!

Perhaps he knew then that the blind would some-day have their libraries and would stand with pride in a sighted world. For Louis Braille had learned, even as a boy, that fingers can "see" in place of eyes and that the touch of words can stir the soul, glad-den the heart, and fill up the darkness with light.

Bibliography

DeGering, Etta B. *Seeing Fingers:* The Story of Louis
Braille. New York: David McKay Co., 1962.
Elliot, John. *The Way of the Tumbrils.* New York: Reynal
& Co., 1958.
Farrell, Gabriel. *The Story of Blindness.* Cambridge: Harvard University Press, 1956.
Freedman, Russell. *Teenagers Who Made History.* New
York: Holiday House, 1961.
Keller, Helen. "Light-Bearer to the World of Darkness."
New York Times Magazine, January 6, 1952, p. 16.
Kugelmass, J. Alvin. *Louis Braille:* Windows for the Blind.
New York: Julian Messner, 1951.
Pinkney, David H. *Napoleon III and the Rebuilding of
Paris.* Princeton: Princeton University Press, 1958.
Roberto, Brother, C.S.C. *Treasures at My Finger Tips:* A
Story of Louis Braille. Notre Dame: Dujarie Press, 1961.
Roblin, Jean. *Louis Braille.* London: Royal National Institute for the Blind, 1960.
Roblin, Jean. *The Reading Fingers:* Life of Louis Braille.
New York: American Foundation for the Blind, 1955.
Ross, Ishbel. *Journey into the Light:* The Story of the Education of the Blind. New York: Appleton-Century-Crofts,
1951.

Sedillot, Rene. *An Outline of French History.* New York: Alfred A. Knopf, 1953.

Webster, Gary. *Journey into Light:* The Story of Louis Braille. New York: Hawthorn Books, 1964.

Wymer, Norman. *Louis Braille.* London: Oxford University Press, 1954.